ISO 9000 Guidelines for the Chemical and Process Industries

Also available from ASQC Quality Press

Specifications for the Chemical and Process Industries:
A Manual for Development and Use
ASQC Chemical and Process Industries Division,
Chemical Interest Committee

Quality Assurance for the Chemical and Process Industries:
A Manual of Good Practices
ASQC Chemical and Process Industries Division,
Chemical Interest Committee

ANSI/ISO/ASQC Q9000-1994 Series: Quality Management
and Quality Assurance Standards

To request a complimentary catalog of publications, call 800-248-1946.

ISO 9000 Guidelines for the Chemical and Process Industries

Second Edition

ASQC Chemical and Process Industries Division

Chemical Interest Committee

ASQC Quality Press
Milwaukee, Wisconsin

ISO 9000 Guidelines for the Chemical and Process Industries, Second Edition
ASQC Chemical and Process Industries Division, Chemical Interest Committee

Library of Congress Cataloging-in-Publication Data

ISO 9000 guidelines for the chemical and process industries / ASQC
  Chemical and Process Industries Division, Chemical Interest
  Committee—2nd ed.
       p. cm.
    Rev. ed. of: ANSI/ASQC Q90/ISO 9000. c1992.
    Includes bibliographical references and index.
    ISBN 0-87389-352-2
    1. Chemical industry—Quality control—Standards.   I. American
  Society for Quality Control. Chemical Interest Committee.
  II. ANSI/ASQC Q90/ISO 9000.
  TP149.A6   1996
  660'.068'5—dc20   95-52155
                                                                      CIP

© 1996 by ASQC

All rights reserved. No part of this book may be reproduced in any form or by any means, electronic, mechanical, photocopying, recording, or otherwise, without the prior written permission of the publisher.

10 9 8 7 6 5 4 3 2 1

ISBN 0-87389-352-2

Acquisitions Editor: Susan Westergard
Project Editor: Jeanne W. Bohn

ASQC Mission: To facilitate continuous improvement and increase customer satisfaction by identifying, communicating, and promoting the use of quality principles, concepts, and technologies; and thereby be recognized throughout the world as the leading authority on, and champion for, quality.

Attention: Schools and Corporations
ASQC Quality Press books, audiotapes, videotapes, and software are available at quantity discounts with bulk purchases for business, educational, or instructional use. For information, please contact ASQC Quality Press at 800-248-1946, or write to ASQC Quality Press, P.O. Box 3005, Milwaukee, WI 53201-3005.

For a free copy of the ASQC Quality Press Publications Catalog, including ASQC membership information, call 800-248-1946.

Printed in the United States of America

    Printed on acid-free recycled paper

ASQC
Quality Press
611 East Wisconsin Avenue
Milwaukee, Wisconsin 53202

Contents

Preface vii
Acknowledgments xvii

4.1	Management Responsibility	1
4.2	Quality System	9
4.3	Contract Review	17
4.4	Design Control	23
4.5	Document and Data Control	33
4.6	Purchasing	39
4.7	Control of Customer-Supplied Product	49
4.8	Product Identification and Traceability	51
4.9	Process Control	55
4.10	Inspection and Testing	61
4.11	Control of Inspection, Measuring, and Test Equipment	71
4.12	Inspection and Test Status	81
4.13	Control of Nonconforming Product	85
4.14	Corrective and Preventive Action	91
4.15	Handling, Storage, Packaging, Preservation, and Delivery	99
4.16	Control of Quality Records	107
4.17	Internal Quality Audits	111

4.18 Training... 117
4.19 Servicing.. 119
4.20 Statistical Techniques 121

Appendix A: Sources for Ordering Standards 125
Appendix B: Acronyms 127
Appendix C: Standards... 129

Glossary 135
Bibliography 141
Index 143

Preface

The Chemical Interest Committee (CIC) of the Chemical and Process Industries Division of the American Society for Quality Control (ASQC) has prepared these guidelines. The intent is to provide guidance in using the American National Standard ANSI/ISO/ASQC Q9001-1994 (ISO 9001) and to promote the use of the Q9000–Q9004 standards in the chemical and process industries. In addition, these guidelines contain examples and good quality practices that may aid in developing effective quality systems.

This second edition has been updated to conform to the 1994 ANSI/ISO/ASQC Q9000 revisions. The authors have captured new knowledge based on the last three years of industry experience in using these guidelines to apply the standard. New to this edition are an updated glossary and appendices including a descriptive matrix of the quality management standards, ordering information, and a list of acronyms.

These guidelines are not intended to be used as a supplemental standard or to modify or alter the standard in any way.

The CIC acknowledges the use of resource materials provided by the following organizations.

> International Organization for Standardization (ISO), Technical Committee on Quality Assurance (TC-176) ISO 9000-1994 series

ASQC Chemical and Process Industries Division, CIC, *Quality Assurance for the Chemical and Process Industries: A Manual of Good Practices*

ASQC, ANSI/ISO/ASQC Q9000–Q9004 quality standards

Purpose

If your company is in the chemical or process industry (CPI) or is a supplier to the CPI, this guide will help you apply the national quality system models, ANSI/ISO/ASQC Q9000-1994 through Q9004-1994. This system directly matches the international quality system known as ISO 9000–9004. There are at least two reasons for using this guide.

- It includes activities that directly or indirectly bear on the quality of your products and services (for example, quality planning, procedures, process control, training, audits, system reviews, and documentation).
- It provides useful interpretation of the meaning of Q9001 specifically for the chemical and process industries. Q9001 originally focused on mechanical industries, and some provisions require interpretation in CPI terms. Much of the guidance is useful for any industry, not just the CPI.

Basic Concepts

As stated in ANSI/ISO/ASQC Q9000-1, an organization should

1. Achieve, maintain, and seek to continuously improve the quality of its products in relationship to the requirements for quality
2. Improve the quality of its own operations so as to continually meet all customers' and other stakeholders' stated and implied needs
3. Provide confidence to its internal managers and other employees that the requirements for quality are being fulfilled and maintained, and that quality improvement is taking place
4. Provide confidence to customers and other stakeholders that the requirements for quality are being, or will be, achieved in the delivered product
5. Provide confidence that quality-system requirements are fulfilled

History

The International Organization for Standardization (ISO) issued the ISO 9000 series documents in 1987. Although they were the first quality-related guidelines published by ISO, they broke no new ground. Rather, they distilled tried and proven quality practices. What made them instantly attractive was that they were rapidly adopted by many nations. They were a comprehensive set of standards and guidelines for a quality system. ISO intended that they would be used as standards by the marketplace, where customers would write contracts requiring suppliers to meet the provisions of 9001, 9002, or 9003.

In 1987 the United States adopted an identical set of standards using American terms. The United Kingdom has adopted the same standards as BS5750, and many other countries have endorsed the same, or similar, standards under various designations. Officials in the European Community saw that the ISO guidelines could set common standards for the quality system features used by a supplier organization in any member country. They adopted the ISO guidelines as EN 29000–29004. As of September 1995, more than 80 countries reported ISO 9000–certification activities. In summary, this quality model has received broad worldwide support.

A revision to the series was approved internationally and in the United States in 1994. The intent of the revision was to clarify requirements and eliminate redundancies. There are many who believe this strengthened the standard.

As part of the revision, Q9002 was made identical to Q9001 except for the omission of the design control section. Q9003 was strengthened substantially and now more closely matches Q9001 except that clauses 4.4, 4.6, 4.9, and 4.19 are not requirements. Paragraph numbering is now the same in Q9001, Q9002, and Q9003.

If you are familiar with quality standards such as FDA GMP, MIL STD 9858A, Ford Q101, or API Q-1, you probably have an understanding of many of the systems required by ANSI/ISO/ASQC Q9001.

The Standards

The five documents in the Q9000 series are a linked set; the ISO 9000 series has identical linkages. Figure P-1 shows the interrelationship of the five main documents.

	Quality Assurance				QM guidance:	Road map:
ANSI/ISO/ASQC Q9001-1994	Requirements: ANSI/ISO/ASQC Q9002-1994	ANSI/ISO/ASQC Q9003-1994	Application guide: ANSI/ISO/ASQC Q9000-2	Clause title in ANSI/ISO/ASQC Q9001-1994	ANSI/ISO/ASQC Q9004-1-1994	ANSI/ISO/ASQC Q9000-1-1994
4.1 ■	■	○	4.1	Management Responsibility	4	4.1; 4.2; 4.3
4.2 ■	■	○	4.2	Quality System	5	4.4; 4.5; 4.8
4.3 ■	■	■	4.3	Contract Review	X	8
4.4 ■	X	X	4.4	Design Control	8	
4.5 ■	■	■	4.5	Document and Data Control	5.3, 11.5	
4.6 ■	■	X	4.6	Purchasing	9	
4.7 ■	■	■	4.7	Customer-Supplied Product	X	
4.8 ■	■	○	4.8	Product Identification and Traceability	11.2	5
4.9 ■	■	X	4.9	Process Control	10; 11	4.6; 4.7
4.10 ■	■	○	4.10	Inspection and Testing	12	
4.11 ■	■	■	4.11	Control of Inspection, Measuring, and Test Equipment	13	
4.12 ■	■	■	4.12	Inspection and Test Status	11.7	
4.13 ■	■	○	4.13	Control of Nonconforming Product	14	
4.14 ■	■	○	4.14	Corrective and Preventive Action	15	
4.15 ■	■	■	4.15	Handling, Storage, Packaging, Preservation, and Delivery	10.4; 16.1; 16.2	
4.16 ■	■	○	4.16	Control of Quality Records	5.3; 17.2; 17.3	
4.17 ■	■	○	4.17	Internal Quality Audits	5.4	4.9
4.18 ■	■	○	4.18	Training	18.1	5.4
4.19 ■	■	X	4.19	Servicing	16.4	
4.20 ■	■	○	4.20	Statistical Techniques	20	
X	X	X	X	Quality Economics	6	
X	X	X	X	Product Safety	19	
X	X	X	X	Marketing	7	

Key:
■ = Comprehensive requirement
○ = Less-comprehensive requirement than ANSI/ISO/ASQC Q9001-1994 and ANSI/ISO/ASQC Q9002-1994
X = Element not present

Figure P-1. Q9001–Q9004 cross reference.

Q9000-1 (ISO 9000-1) is titled *Quality Management and Quality Assurance Standards—Guidelines for Selection and Use*. It sets forth the principal quality concepts, describes the use of these standards within customer/supplier contracts, and provides guidance in the use of the other four standards.

Q9001–Q9003 (ISO 9001–9003) are standards for quality systems that a customer may contractually require a supplier to meet. These standards are suitable for use in external second-party customer quality assurance agreements. The standards are also used extensively as the basis for independent third-party quality system registrations. Registration is based on a comprehensive audit. The audit team should be competent in both this standard and the industry's issues. Team members will look for objective evidence that your system is documented, implemented, and effective. This may reduce the number of total audits your facility experiences. Registration provides discipline to maintain the system. Registration may provide a marketing advantage.

Details about the standards include

- Q9001 is the most comprehensive. It is appropriate when the contract calls for the supplier to develop, design, produce, install, service, and supply a product or service. All of the requirements of the other two standards (Q9002 and Q9003) are included in Q9001. *This book focuses on Q9001.*

- Q9002 is most appropriate when the contract calls for the supplier to produce, install, service, and supply to an existing design. Only clause 4.4, Design Control, does not apply to Q9002.

- Q9003 applies when the supplier is required to supply based only on final inspection and testing. Clauses 4.4, 4.6, 4.9, and 4.19 do not apply to Q9003, and some other sections have less comprehensive requirements. In the CPI, Q9001 and Q9002 are most frequently used.

The Q9004 and ISO 10000 series of documents include guidance on various aspects of quality management. Q9004-1, in contrast to Q9001–Q9003, is a guideline for *internal* quality management activities. This includes a set of quality elements that any company can use to develop its own internal quality system.

The original intent of the standard was that an organization would focus first on an internal quality system using Q9004, however, the marketplace has seen a shift of emphasis toward third-party certification based on Q9001–Q9003. This has resulted in too little emphasis on true quality improvement. Therefore, organizations are encouraged to closely examine the guidelines (not requirements) contained in Q9004 with an eye toward improvement rather than certification. Please note, however, that the primary focus of this book is on Q9001.

Q9004-3 is a guideline for internal quality management activities specifically for the CPI. At present, this guideline is still based on the 1987 version of the standards. There are other guidance documents that are not treated in this book. A listing is included in appendix C.

How to Use This Guide

We have translated Q9001 into language used by the CPI. The intent is to provide comprehensive coverage of all elements of the standard, even though some parts may not appear to have relevance to all CPI companies. This book does not interpret clauses 0.0, 1.0, and 2.0 in the standard because the information in these clauses is self-explanatory.

There are three special terms that are used consistently in the standard. This book uses these terms in the same sense as the standard's authors intended. To avoid confusion, it will be worthwhile to become familiar with these terms (see Figure P-2).

- *Supplier* refers to the company establishing a quality system and producing the product covered by the standard. You, as the user of this guide, will frequently be the supplier.

- *Subcontractor* refers to any provider of purchased products (for example, raw materials, in-bound goods, utilities, or equipment) or services (for example, maintenance or packaging) that come into the supplier's company (organization, plant, or process). Toll processors, contract warehouses, laboratories, packagers, calibration services, and repackagers are examples of subcontractors, whether internal or external. The word *subsupplier* is synonymous with subcontractor.

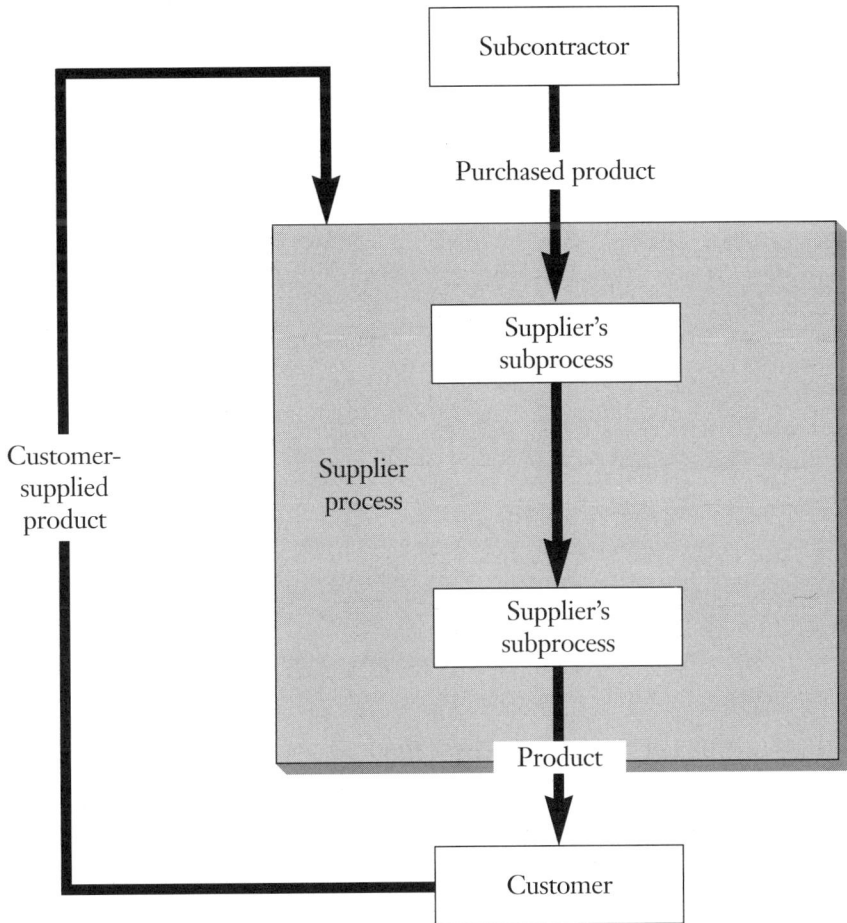

Figure P-2. Q9000 terminology.

Operations internal to a supplier company should be regarded as subcontractors if they are outside the quality system defined by the supplier. A key to implementation and registration is the scope of the quality system as defined by the supplier. Internal suppliers must be considered when drafting the scope.

- *Customer* refers to the company (organization, plant, or division) receiving the supplier's products.

Three definitions in Q9001 are particularly worth noting.

product: Result of activities or processes.
—A product may include service, hardware, processed materials, software, or a combination thereof.
—A product can be tangible (e.g., assemblies or processed materials) or intangible (e.g., knowledge or concepts), or a combination thereof.
—For the purposes of this American National Standard, the term "product" applies to the intended product offering only and not to unintended by-products affecting the environment. This differs from the definition given in ANSI/ISO/ASQC A8402-1994.

tender: Offer made by a supplier in response to an invitation to satisfy a contract award to provide product.

contract; accepted order: Agreed requirements between a supplier and customer transmitted by any means.

Other specialized terms used in the Q9000 series are given in the glossary and in ANSI/ISO/ASQC A8402-1994.

Within each section of this guide, the format used to provide the information is

- Introduction.

- The Q9001 clause is stated verbatim in the box.

- What's new in the 1994 version of Q9001. There were basically two types of changes: clarifications of the original intent and new requirements. **Bold type is used in the What's New? section to indicate the more substantive changes.**

- Guidance on applying the clause requirements to the CPI. This is a discussion of CPI-specific issues and good quality practices relating to the element.

- Interpretation of notes in the standard. Notes are advisory, not mandatory.

- Important linkages between parts of the standards.
- Cautions regarding unwritten rules and helpful hints based on insights from experienced users of these standards.
- Differences found in related clauses of Q9003.

Conclusion

The standard has changed somewhat, and the CPI has gained a great deal of experience with Q9000 since the first edition of this book. These changes have been incorporated in this second edition. The authors wish you success in designing your quality system to drive true quality improvement.

Acknowledgments

ASQC and the CPID Chemical Interest Committee appreciate the contributions of the authors of this revision. They are

Jim Bigelow, Exxon Chemical Company
Bill Cox, TQM Consulting
Richard Hoff, Omni Tech International
Gary Lewis, Amoco Polymers, Inc.
Ken Moist, Performance Plus Associates
Rebecca White, ABS Quality Evaluations

We would also like to acknowledge the major contributions of those who wrote the original version of this text. They are

Jim Bigelow	Norman Knowlden
Frank Bondurant	James Krueger
Bradford Brown	Perce Ness
Georgia Kay Carter	Bill Ochs
Don Engelstad	Chris Ostman
David Files	Anil Parikh
Peter Fortini	Philip Parker
Dwight Grimestad	Frank Sinibaldi
Richard Hoff	Jack Weiler
Rudy Kittlitz	

The committee would also like to thank Jan Dunbar and Ingrid Caballero of Exxon Chemical Company for their administrative support. In addition, the committee is grateful to the following people who reviewed the manuscript for Quality Press at various stages, providing feedback to enhance content and ensure accuracy.

Charles A. Cianfrani, Elsag Bailey Process Automation
Ian G. Durand, Service Process Consulting Inc.
Donald W. Marquardt, Donald W. Marquardt and Associates
Joseph J. Tsiakals, Baxter Healthcare Laboratories

4.1

Management Responsibility

Introduction

This clause of the standard deals with senior managers' leadership of, involvement in, and commitment to quality.

> Q9001-1994 standard
> **4.1 MANAGEMENT RESPONSIBILITY**
> **4.1.1 Quality policy**
> The supplier's management with executive responsibility shall define and document its policy for quality, including objectives for quality and its commitment to quality. The quality policy shall be relevant to the supplier's organizational goals and the expectations and needs of its customers. The supplier shall ensure that this policy is understood, implemented, and maintained at all levels of the organization.

What's New?

- Senior management shall define the quality policy and objectives, and document how commitment to quality is demonstrated.

Guidance

The supplier's executive management shall develop a quality policy statement. The quality policy is the overall statement about the supplier's policy and direction concerning quality, as formally expressed by top management. The quality policy may also contain the mission, vision, and guidelines necessary to demonstrate the supplier's commitment to these values.

Objectives for and commitments to quality need to be documented in some form, either in the quality manual or supporting documentation such as yearly company objectives. Performance against these objectives should be measured and reviewed as part of a continuous improvement process.

It is an unwritten rule that the policy statement should be signed and dated by the most senior executive as the first step in implementing the supplier's quality system. This policy should be included in the quality manual. The supplier's management is responsible for communicating the quality policy throughout the organization and for reinforcing organization-wide ownership of the quality values through day-to-day actions. All employees need to understand the quality policy and how it affects them and their role in the quality system.

The quality policy does not need to restate the organization's goals and expectations of its customers, but the relationships should be evident.

Q9001-1994 standard

4.1.2 Organization

4.1.2.1 Responsibility and authority

The responsibility, authority, and the interrelation of personnel who manage, perform, and verify work affecting quality shall be defined and documented, particularly for personnel who need the organizational freedom and authority to:

a) initiate action to prevent the occurrence of any nonconformities relating to product, process, and quality system;

b) identify and record any problems relating to the product, process, and quality system;

c) initiate, recommend, or provide solutions through designated channels;

d) verify the implementation of solutions;

e) control further processing, delivery, or installation of nonconforming product until the deficiency or unsatisfactory condition has been corrected.

What's New?

- Responsibility and authority shall be documented.

Guidance

Management needs to clearly define and document the responsibilities, authorities, and interfaces of all personnel who in any way affect the quality of the product, process, or quality system. An organizational chart is often used to show responsible functions and critical interfaces of personnel who carry out the activities identified in items (a) through (e). This chart should show functions and does not need to duplicate the supplier's overall hierarchical organizational chart.

To facilitate document maintenance, an organizational chart should include titles, not individuals' names. Many organizations use job descriptions that define the functional responsibilities and authority by job title. Alternatively, responsibility and authority may be defined in individual procedures. These, however, should refer to other documentation that can identify the current position holders.

Individuals responsible for quality-related actions must have the authority to take those actions in a timely and complete manner.

This clause in Q9003 is limited to personnel engaged in final inspection and/or test.

> **Q9001-1994 standard**
>
> **4.1.2.2 Resources**
>
> The supplier shall identify resource requirements and provide adequate resources, including the assignment of trained personnel (see 4.18), for management, performance of work, and verification activities including internal quality audits.

What's New?

- The clause's scope has been expanded to include identification of resource requirements for management and performance of work.

Guidance

This requirement says the supplier shall provide *all the resources* (equipment, personnel, and time) needed to operate its defined quality system effectively. Resources must be identified and provided for management of the system, defined work, and verification that activities have occurred as planned. Some examples include equipment, material, time, facilities, people, training, and technology.

Verification activities may include: inspection, test, design, process monitoring, and auditing. Audits shall be carried out "by personnel independent of those having direct responsibility for the work being performed" according to clause 4.17. The internal quality audit is a major tool for the verification of the adequacy of resources and training.

> **Q9001-1994 standard**
>
> **4.1.2.3 Management representative**
>
> The supplier's management with executive responsibility shall appoint a member of the supplier's own management who, irrespective of other responsibilities, shall have defined authority for
>
> a) ensuring that a quality system is established, implemented, and maintained in accordance with this American National Standard, and

b) reporting on the performance of the quality system to the supplier's management for review and as a basis for improvement of the quality system.

NOTE 5 The responsibility of a management representative may also include liaison with external parties on matters relating to the supplier's quality system.

What's New?

- Senior managers are responsible for appointing one of their own staff to have authority for the quality system.
- The management representative must provide information on the performance of the quality system for management review.

Guidance

The supplier's management representative will generally be a high-ranking individual or, at minimum, have direct access to senior management. This individual cannot be from outside the organization, such as a consultant or contractor, and needs to be knowledgeable enough about the quality system to perform these functions. The management representative may function as the quality assurance interface with the customer, subcontractors, and external registration bodies. The representative should oversee the supplier's compliance with all aspects of the standard. The standard does not require this person to devote full time to this responsibility as long as other assigned activities do not restrict the authority and opportunity to ensure compliance with the standard. The management representative may designate others to handle specific facets of the compliance program.

Q9001-1994 standard

4.1.3 Management review

The supplier's management with executive responsibility shall review the quality system at defined intervals sufficient to ensure its continuing

> suitability and effectiveness in satisfying the requirements of this American National Standard and the supplier's stated quality policy and objectives (see 4.1.1). Records of such reviews shall be maintained (see 4.16).

What's New?
- The management review interval must now be defined in the quality system.

Guidance

This is one of the most important requirements of the standard. Management must ensure that the quality system is working effectively and reflects current conditions. This requires that executive managers conduct quality reviews.

Although it is not specifically required by the standard, the supplier's managers should formally review the operation of the entire quality system at least annually. Some companies integrate these reviews into their overall business reviews. More frequent reviews, say quarterly or monthly, are recommended. When major changes to the quality system have been made, interim reviews may be required.

Records of the review must be maintained and should include results, needed preventive and corrective actions, and assignment of responsibilities. Subsequent reviews should examine the effectiveness of such actions. Reviews must include

- Policy
- Objectives
- Internal audits
- Preventive actions
- Corrective actions

Reviews might also include

- Resources (people, equipment, time, funding)
- Complaints
- Statistical measures of quality
- Follow-up from prior management reviews
- Measurements of returns, rework, and waste levels

Participants in the management review should include representatives from all relevant functions affected by the quality system.

4.2

Quality System

Introduction

This clause of the standard defines the requirements for the supplier's quality system. The standard requires the supplier to have a documented quality system. Read Q9004-1 clauses 4.4 to 5.3 for a complete discussion of quality systems. Two definitions from those clauses are cited.

- A quality system is the organizational structure, procedures, processes, and resources for implementing quality management.

- The quality system typically applies to, and interacts with, all activities pertinent to the quality of a product. It will involve all phases in the life-cycle of a product and processes, from initial identification of market needs to final satisfaction of requirements.

> **Q9001-1994 standard**
>
> **4.2 QUALITY SYSTEM**
>
> **4.2.1 General**
>
> The supplier shall establish, document, and maintain a quality system as a means of ensuring that product conforms to specified requirements. The supplier shall prepare a quality manual covering the requirements of this American National Standard. The quality manual shall include or make reference to the quality-system procedures and outline the structure of the documentation used in the quality system.
>
> NOTE 6 Guidance on quality manuals is given in ISO 10013.

What's New?

- **A quality manual is now required that includes or references documented procedures.**
- **The quality manual must outline the structure of the quality system documentation and reference quality system procedures.**
- Reference to ISO 10013 has been added.

Guidance

The standard requires that the quality system be documented, demonstrating that a formal, organized quality system is in place and providing an authoritative description of the system. The required method of documenting the organization of a quality system is through a quality manual. The quality manual is the directory of the quality system. It should describe the company's policies, specify responsibilities, and identify or refer to related procedures that complement the quality manual and provide more detail on the quality system. For a small company, the manual could be the collection of procedures themselves.

The quality manual may be corporate or divisional, or it may describe a specific process within a manufacturing site. It is important that the quality manual define the scope of the quality system. The quality manual must cover every element within the scope of the quality system.

> ### Q9001-1994 standard
> **4.2.2 Quality-system procedures**
>
> The supplier shall
>
> a) prepare documented procedures consistent with the requirements of this American National Standard and the supplier's stated quality policy, and
>
> b) effectively implement the quality system and its documented procedures.
>
> For the purposes of this American National Standard, the range and detail of the procedures that form part of the quality system shall be dependent upon the complexity of the work, the methods used, and the skills and training needed by personnel involved in carrying out the activity.
>
> NOTE 7 Documented procedures may make reference to work instructions that define how an activity is performed.

What's New?

- The standard now recognizes that there are variations in complexity of quality systems used by different types and sizes of organizations.
- Note 7 is new.

Guidance

A documented quality system may use the concept of tiered documentation. This is structured so that detail is increased in lower tiers. The top tier is the quality manual, while the lower tiers are procedures and work instructions. Records (see 4.16) provide objective evidence that the policies, procedures, and instructions have been implemented. Refer to clause 4.16, Control of Quality Records.

At a minimum, the quality manual should address all the requirements in the standard and any other standards related to quality systems as appropriate for the industry and for the supplier (for example, current good manufacturing practices [GMP]), and how these requirements will be met. The manual could refer to related policies and procedures such as

- Business mission, quality policy
- Specifications
- Customer service practices
- Industry-specific requirements
- Manufacturing methods
- Warranties and guarantees
- Process control
- Housekeeping, safety, environmental concerns

The standard explicitly requires the supplier to document quality system procedures. The quality system procedures and instructions should be effectively implemented, as evidenced by quality records such as

- Internal quality audit reports
- Quantitative measures of performance (objectives for quality)
- Management review of the quality system

The quality manual forms the top tier of the quality system documentation (see Figure 4.2-1). It details goals and the organization's policies. These should be in line with customer requirements. A very popular means of documenting a quality manual is to divide the quality manual into 20 sections based on the ANSI/ISO/ASQC Q9001 clauses (although this is not a requirement). Each section details a quality policy and refers to procedures established to fulfill the goals set in the quality manual.

The second tier consists of site or departmental quality system procedures. These procedures cover the major aspects of work done within the plant and include the quality system elements required to meet the ANSI/ISO/ASQC Q9000 criteria and customers' requirements. The departmental procedures that are relevant under the ANSI/ISO/ASQC Q9000 guidelines must be referenced in the quality system manual.

The third tier consists of work instructions, manufacturing instructions, standard operating procedures (SOPs), department-specific procedures, and quality inspection plans. Work instructions or manufacturing instructions are detailed instructions on how a product is made and are

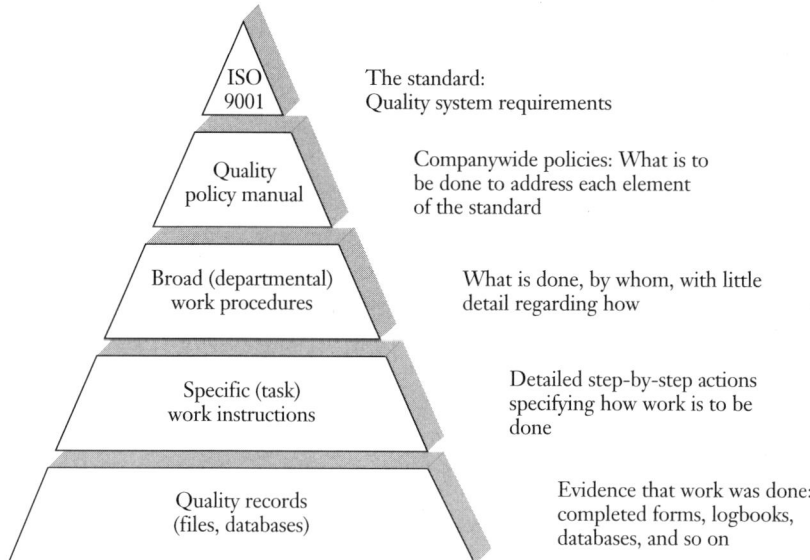

Figure 4.2-1. Quality system document levels.

specific to an operating unit. Each operating unit has its own manual of manufacturing instructions containing step-by-step descriptions of activities that must be performed at various stages of manufacturing.

Quality plan documents set out the required quality-related activities specific to a product or a group of products. They include references to raw materials, intermediates and finished product quality inspection and test requirements, sampling plans, and other quality procedures related to verification of product at appropriate intervals and stages of production.

Q9001-1994 standard

4.2.3 Quality planning

The supplier shall define and document how the requirements for quality will be met. Quality planning shall be consistent with all other requirements of a supplier's quality system and shall be documented in a format to suit the supplier's method of operation. The supplier shall give consideration to the following activities, as appropriate, in meeting the specified requirements for products, projects, or contracts:

a) the preparation of quality plans;

b) the identification and acquisition of any controls, processes, equipment (including inspection and test equipment), fixtures, resources, and skills that may be needed to achieve the required quality;

c) ensuring the compatibility of the design, the production process, installation, servicing, inspection and test procedures, and the applicable documentation;

d) the updating, as necessary, of quality control, inspection, and testing techniques, including the development of new instrumentation;

e) the identification of any measurement requirement involving capability that exceeds the known state of the art, in sufficient time for the needed capability to be developed;

f) the identification of suitable verification at appropriate stages in the realization of product;

g) the clarification of standards of acceptability for all features and requirements, including those which contain a subjective element;

h) the identification and preparation of quality records (see 4.16).

NOTE 8 The quality plans referred to (see 4.2.3a) may be in the form of a reference to the appropriate documented procedures that form an integral part of the supplier's quality system.

What's New?

- **The requirement for quality planning has been added along with guidance as to what should be considered when creating these plans. What was once a note is now a requirement.**

Guidance

The intent of the standard is for the supplier to define in concrete terms the tactical side of how quality will be achieved. This clause does not require strategic planning as might be referenced in the Malcolm Baldrige National Quality Award. Considerable latitude is available as to how a plan might be created and what its content should be based on the nature of the company's business.

The requirements in this section are that the supplier define and document how the organization will meet all quality and customer requirements. Many of these elements will be defined during contract review and design control processes.

At a minimum, many companies already have existing systems in place that define and document how the product will be inspected and tested at various stages of production: receiving, in-process, and final inspection and testing. Therefore, verification activities should include documented procedures or quality plans that define where, when, what, how, and who will carry out these activities. Examples include the following:

- What tests are to be done
- What requirements or specifications must be met
- How often the tests should be done
- By what functions the tests should be performed
- Where in the process the tests should be performed

Subclauses (a) through (h) state considerations for these activities "as appropriate," and, therefore, are not required, depending on the nature of the supplier's business. A quality plan would define the requirements to successfully produce and verify that the product meets customer requirements and could consider the following as appropriate.

- Resources
- Materials
- Process equipment
- Controls
- Manufacturing equipment

- Test equipment
- Test materials
- Training needed
- Sampling plans

A quality plan should be updated whenever changes to customer requirements take place or whenever a new product is introduced. The design of new products would normally include creation of a quality plan in the output phase (clause 4.4.5) to show what factors are essential in producing a quality product.

It is often useful to show a flowchart/block diagram of the process flow with key inspection and test points in the quality manual or related procedures. The quality plans or procedures that relate to the required inspection or tests could also be referenced as part of the diagram. Quality plans will normally identify the quality records that should be kept to provide objective evidence of conformance. More guidance on quality plans is available in ISO/DIS 9004-5, *Guidelines for Quality Plans*.

4.3

Contract Review

Introduction

This clause of the standard covers the procedures a supplier uses to ensure that it understands and is capable of meeting the customer's requirements. It is not to be confused with the handling of contracts between the supplier and its subcontractors, which is governed by clause 4.6. (See Figure 4.3-1.)

Two definitions that are important to the interpretation of this clause were added to section 3 of the 1994 version of Q9001.

- **3.2 tender:** Offer made by a supplier in response to an invitation to satisfy a contract award to provide product.

- **3.3 contract; accepted order:** Agreed requirements between a supplier and customer transmitted by any means.

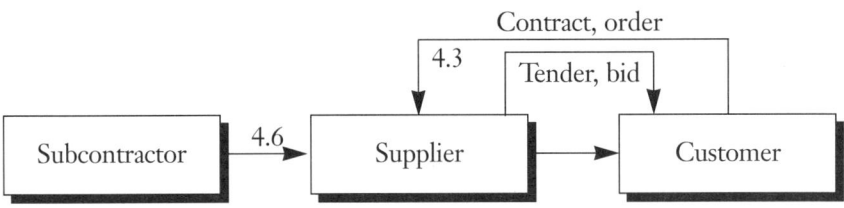

Figure 4.3-1. Contract review is with the customer, not the subcontractor.

> **Q9001-1994 standard**
>
> ### 4.3 CONTRACT REVIEW
>
> **4.3.1 General**
>
> The supplier shall establish and maintain documented procedures for contract review and for the coordination of these activities.
>
> **4.3.2 Review**
>
> Before submission of a tender, or at the acceptance of a contract or order (statement of requirement), the tender, contract, or order shall be reviewed by the supplier to ensure that:
>
> a) the requirements are adequately defined and documented; where no written statement of requirement is available for an order received by verbal means, the supplier shall ensure that the order requirements are agreed before their acceptance;
>
> b) any differences between the contract or accepted order requirements and those in the tender are resolved;
>
> c) the supplier has the capability to meet the contract or accepted order requirements.

What's New?

- **Definitions were added for *tender* and for *contract* or *accepted order*.**
- **The standard now makes provision for handling verbal orders.**

Guidance

The supplier must review, understand, and document all of the customer's requirements. The supplier must then ensure its ability to meet all of these contract terms. For the purposes of this standard, a contract can be anything from a formal document to an oral request. A contract can cover, for example,

- A price quote or request for proposal
- A single shipment

- Multiple shipments
- An order received against an annual forecasted quantity
- A release for shipment against an annual contract

The supplier should have a system with documented procedures to ensure that

- The customer's requirements are absolutely clear. Ideally, these requirements are documented, but verbal orders are acceptable as long as the requirements are understood and agreed prior to acceptance. Even in the case of a verbal request, there is generally some form of documentation internal to the supplier that should satisfy the requirement for records of contract review in clause 4.3.4.

- Any differences between the order and the original inquiry are resolved and agreed upon. Likewise, discrepancies between the supplier's original quote and the customer's eventual order must be resolved.

- The supplier is capable of meeting all of the customer's requirements. This includes having the capability to

    —Meet the product specifications

    —Meet the quantity and delivery time requirements

    —Measure the product parameters according to required methods (for example, ASTM) and to the required degree of accuracy and precision

    —Meet any special requirements, such as unique packaging, labeling, unloading, or delivery requirements

Note that this use of the word *capability* does not necessarily carry with it the connotation of statistical capability indices such as C_{pk} or P_{pk}. If such measures are part of the contract or are otherwise required by the supplier's own management, then clause 4.20 would apply.

Contract review procedures should be integrated with other applicable elements of the quality system, particularly considering

- Quality planning, clause 4.2.3
- Design input, clause 4.4.4

- Customer-supplied product, clause 4.7
- Final inspection and testing, clause 4.10.4
- Measurement accuracy and precision, clause 4.11.2a
- Handling, storage, packaging, preservation, and delivery, clause 4.15

In reviewing and accepting an order, several issues should be addressed.

- The essential features of each order such as quantity, price, payment terms and conditions, specifications, packaging requirements, documentation (for example, certificates of analysis, material safety data sheets), government regulations, delivery points, and special unloading requirements need to be confirmed and transmitted to those who need the information to fill the order.

- The production schedule for multigrade or multiproduct plants must take into account stock levels, storage capacity, forecasted sales demand, run length, and maintenance shutdowns.

- The custody transfer point in the delivery process at which responsibility for maintaining the quality of product passes from the supplier to the customer (or other party) must be identified. In the case of consignment stocks, responsibility for the preservation of quality needs to be defined and agreed upon in the contract. This is especially important in the case where a distributor is acting as the customer or subcontractor, and when the product is supplied via shared pipeline facilities, rather than unique shipping containers.

- When special customer requirements exist, the supplier must be able to meet these requirements. The system or quality plan should ensure that such special requirements are known to all involved in processing the order.

Meeting the needs of the customer requires systems and procedures that facilitate direct communication and teamwork among the sales, marketing, manufacturing, and shipping functions of the supplier.

For a product exchange agreement or for a toll processor, the parties need to define their respective responsibilities with regard to Q9001 issues. All elements of the standard should be considered in any exchange or tolling agreement (see clause 4.7).

> Q9001-1994 standard
>
> **4.3.3 Amendment to contract**
>
> The supplier shall identify how an amendment to a contract is made and correctly transferred to the functions concerned within the supplier's organization.
>
> **4.3.4 Records**
>
> Records of contract reviews shall be maintained (see 4.16).
>
> NOTE 9 Channels for communication and interfaces with the customer's organization in these contract matters should be established.

What's New?

- **The standard has added requirements for contract amendments and for communicating such changes within the organization.**
- Note 9 is new.

Guidance

How changes in the contract will be made, whether initiated by customer or supplier, needs to be addressed. The change process needs to provide for communication of the change. Such changes might include specifications, tolerance limits, quantities, or delivery dates.

Tenders, quotes, proposals, orders, contracts, and records of contract reviews are important elements of the quality system and should be controlled in the same manner as other records (see clause 4.16). These records should clearly show review and approval of orders and contracts.

Note 9 in the standard is particularly relevant to the CPI. Whenever appropriate, establish a dialogue between customer and supplier regarding customer's requirements. This is especially important in the case where a large manufacturer with multiple plants and a centralized marketing function defines internal customer–supplier relationships between the manufacturing plants and the marketing organization, rather than the external customer.

4.4

Design Control

Introduction

This clause of the standard is referenced when product development or design is undertaken. When process design/development occurs in conjunction with product development, these requirements may also be applied, in accordance with the supplier's stated plans. In any case, the process must be operated under "controlled conditions," per clause 4.9.

Conformance with the requirements of this clause is required when product development is contractual in nature. Otherwise, implementation of this clause is at the discretion of the supplier and may still add value through added structure and formalization.

In the chemical and process industries, design is typically in the form of new product development and the associated process design. In many cases, new products are developed to be manufactured with existing equipment. The requirements of this clause are rigorous and very structured. Therefore, many CPI companies have avoided this clause by narrowing the scope of their system to Q9002, which does not include clause 4.4, Design Control.

> Q9001-1994 standard
>
> ## 4.4 DESIGN CONTROL
>
> ### 4.4.1 General
>
> The supplier shall establish and maintain documented procedures to control and verify the design of the product in order to ensure that the specified requirements are met.

What's New?

- The standard includes clarification that procedures must be documented.

Guidance

When product designs are complete, the results should be implemented into the quality system through quality plans (clause 4.2.3), process control (clause 4.9), and document changes (clause 4.5.3). If the development of a new or modified product, process, or application involves a contractual agreement, a thorough contract review in accordance with the requirements of clause 4.3 must be completed and recorded. Design control requirements are not included in Q9002 or Q9003. If product or process design and development are not conducted, Q9002 should be considered for implementation.

> Q9001-1994 standard
>
> ### 4.4.2 Design and development planning
>
> The supplier shall prepare plans for each design and development activity. The plans shall describe or reference these activities, and define responsibility for their implementation. The design and development activities shall be assigned to qualified personnel equipped with adequate resources. The plans shall be updated, as the design evolves.

What's New?

- Personnel must be qualified and have adequate resources.
- The previous clause 4.4.2.1 was absorbed into the revised 4.4.2.

Guidance

Comprehensive planning for design activities includes research, development, scale-up, and introduction of a new product, application, service, or process. The plans will be specific to each project. Plans specify the groups within the organization (and outside subcontractors) responsible for various aspects of the development, input data required for their work, resources they will require and results to be generated, stages at which project reviews (see 4.4.6) will be held, and so on. Personnel involved in a project should be qualified (see clause 4.18) by education, training, and/or experience. They should receive adequate time, funding, and support to carry out the tasks assigned.

It is understood that many aspects of a project will depend on results not available at the time of initial planning. This means that plans should be reviewed and updated during the course of the project so that nothing falls through the cracks.

The supplier's plan should consider all elements specifically addressed in the customer's contract (see clause 4.3), which may include:

- Requirements for product performance, quantity, packaging
- Possible modifications to the customer's process
- Process engineering, such as process conditions and controls
- Engineering issues, such as construction design and development
- Quality control including specifications for raw materials, intermediates, and final products; measurement procedures and sampling plans
- Need for field evaluation
- Safety and environment issues
- Regulatory issues
- Documentation required

> Q9001-1994 standard
>
> **4.4.3 Organizational and technical interfaces**
>
> Organizational and technical interfaces between different groups which input into the design process shall be defined and the necessary information documented, transmitted, and regularly reviewed.

What's New?

- Interfaces must now be defined, not just identified.

Guidance

Good communication is essential for good development and design. The planning process should ensure that necessary information is documented and communicated among the groups involved, both internal and external. Interfacing is typically required among personnel in the areas of sales, marketing, research, engineering, quality assurance, purchasing, production, technical service, and regulatory, as well as subcontractors of equipment, raw materials, and services.

> Q9001-1994 standard
>
> **4.4.4 Design input**
>
> Design-input requirements relating to the product, including applicable statutory and regulatory requirements, shall be identified, documented, and their selection reviewed by the supplier for adequacy. Incomplete, ambiguous, or conflicting requirements shall be resolved with those responsible for imposing these requirements.
>
> Design input shall take into consideration the results of any contract-review activities.

What's New?

- The requirement for conformance with applicable statutory and regulatory requirements were moved from the Design output section.
- **A direct connection between design input and contract review was added.**

Guidance

Project objectives should be adequately defined, documented, and clear to all involved. Any applicable statutory requirements must be included in the input to the design process. This is especially crucial in the CPI, where safety and environmental regulations abound.

In many CPI projects, a detailed and specific definition of design input requirements may not be possible in the early stages, since important characteristics of a material may be impossible to specify until the product is created or has demonstrated its performance in a prospective customer's application. Full-scale process development frequently begins only after the testing of relatively small quantities has created a market for the product.

Full specification of the product may even depend on data only available from testing of material from the scaled-up process. When this is the case, close cooperation between supplier and customers is especially vital, and ongoing communication of product requirements and process capability should be explicitly planned. Care must be taken to ensure that input to the design process includes all items specified by a customer during contract review (see clause 4.3).

Q9001-1994 standard

4.4.5 Design output

Design output shall be documented and expressed in terms that can be verified against design-input requirements and validated (see 4.4.8).

Design output shall:

a) meet the design-input requirements;

b) contain or make reference to acceptance criteria;

c) identify those characteristics of the design that are crucial to the safe and proper functioning of the product (e.g., operating, storage, handling, maintenance, and disposal requirements).

Design-output documents shall be reviewed before release.

What's New?

- The original intent of verification of design output against design input requirements has been clarified.
- **A requirement for review of design output documents has been added.**

Guidance

The design output documentation should not only define the specifications of the product and process, but also describe in detail the reasoning behind the conception of the product and the design, as well as the planned operation of a process facility. The output of the design process often takes the form of a quality plan or documentation with the following elements.

- Product specifications
- Physical properties, material safety data sheets for products, packaging, and shelf life
- Approved raw materials sources
- Sampling procedures, test methods, and equipment
- Safety and environment factors
- Specifics of equipment, procedures, and processes

The design output must be reviewed to ensure that requirements (a), (b), and (c) of clause 4.4.5 have been met. Participants in the review should include appropriate representatives defined in clause 4.4.3 interfaces. Objective evidence of the review must be recorded (see clause 4.4.6).

Q9001-1994 standard

4.4.6 Design review

At appropriate stages of design, formal documented reviews of the design results shall be planned and conducted. Participants at each design review shall include representatives of all functions concerned with the design stage being reviewed, as well as other specialist personnel, as required. Records of such reviews shall be maintained (see 4.16).

What's New?

- **Design review is now a stand-alone subclause with new, specific requirements.**

Guidance

ANSI/ISO/ASQC A8402-1994 defines *design review* as:

> Documented, comprehensive and systematic examinations of a design to evaluate its capability to fulfill the requirements for quality, identify problems, if any, and propose the development of solutions.
>
> NOTE—A design review can be conducted at any stage of the design process, but should in any case be conducted at the completion of this process.

Design reviews should be held at intervals defined in the design plan. These reviews should verify that design activity results are satisfactory and on schedule. Design reviews should assess progress against the design plan and may indicate the need for design verification. All functions involved in the design process should participate in the design reviews. Records of findings of design reviews must be maintained.

Q9001-1994 standard

4.4.7 Design verification

At appropriate stages of design, design verification shall be performed to ensure that the design-stage output meets the design-stage input requirements. The design-verification measures shall be recorded (see 4.16).

NOTE 10 In addition to conducting design reviews (see 4.4.6), design verification may include activities such as

—performing alternative calculations,

—comparing the new design with a similar proven design, if available,

—undertaking tests and demonstrations, and

—reviewing the design-stage documents before release.

What's New?

- The text of this subclause was considerably reduced. Note 10 was added, which defines various methods of design verification.

Guidance

Design verification is conducted as appropriate to ensure that design results at each stage meet the design input requirements. At the conclusion of each phase of design or development, a documented, systematic verification of the design results should be conducted.

Design verification may be undertaken independently or in support of design reviews by applying methods such as the following:

- Examples of alternative calculations might include graphical versus analytical approaches or empirical versus theoretical solutions.
- Laboratory analyses of appropriate physical properties of bench scale batches, lab prototypes, or models.
- See other examples in note 10.

The results of the final design verification should ensure that the design package documentation is complete and up-to-date. The total document package defining the design should require approval of the functions affected by or contributing to the design. This approval constitutes the production release and authorizes that the design can be realized. Records of design verification must be maintained.

Q9001-1994 standard

4.4.8 Design validation

Design validation shall be performed to ensure that product conforms to defined user needs and/or requirements.

NOTES

11 Design validation follows successful design verification (see 4.4.7).

12 Validation is normally performed under defined operating conditions.

> 13 Validation is normally performed on the final product, but may be necessary in earlier stages prior to product completion.
>
> 14 Multiple validations may be performed if there are different intended uses.

What's New?
- **This is a new subclause added to separate design verification from design validation.**
- Notes 11 through 14 were added for guidance.

Guidance
Following a successful design verification, a validation is performed in order to verify that the final design meets the defined user needs and/or requirements. This validation may take the form of preproduction trials, simulated conditions in a laboratory environment, and field tests or evaluations by customers.

It is sometimes helpful to consider design verification as testing to ensure that the finished product has the specified physical or chemical properties (for example, density, purity, melting point, color, and so on) that are anticipated to fulfill the required function. Conversely, design validation is confirming that the final product performs the required function. If the final product has multiple uses, a design validation should be performed for each. Another way of stating this distinction is

Term	Compares design to
Verification	Documented design input
Validation	Meeting user needs

ANSI/ISO/ASQC A8402-1994 definitions for *verification* and *validation* are included in the glossary.

> **Q9001-1994 standard**
>
> **4.4.9 Design changes**
>
> All design changes and modifications shall be identified, documented, reviewed, and approved by authorized personnel before their implementation.

What's New?

- A minor change was made clarifying that design changes must be approved by authorized personnel.

Guidance

Examples of design changes for which review and documentation requirements apply may include changes to raw materials, product composition or formulation, process conditions or procedures, testing procedures, specifications, packaging, and labels.

Design change procedures should define the company functions that are responsible for review and approval of a given change. Functions may include product management, quality assurance, engineering, development, research, legal, regulatory, and others, as appropriate. When a design change affects a contract requirement, a new contract review may be required (see clause 4.3.4). Customer review of changes may also be appropriate because of the potential for unforeseen product performance effects.

Neither Q9002 nor Q9003 include design control.

4.5

Document and Data Control

Introduction

This clause of the standard covers the requirement for maintaining, revising, and issuing those documents and data that can affect the quality of products. It is important that those who use the documents have the correct information.

Note that there is an important distinction between documents and records. *Documents* are current and future-oriented, such as plans, procedures, policies, and blank forms. As such, they are subject to being revised (see clause 4.5.3). *Records* are past-oriented. Records provide objective evidence that work was done. Examples include completed forms, audit reports, meeting minutes, control charts, and database entries. They are generally not subject to being revised or changed. The requirements of clause 4.5 apply *only* to documents, while clause 4.16 defines requirements for records. Documents may turn into records. As an example, a process batch sheet may describe how the product is to be made and also provide a means for recording actual amounts added or process settings used.

> Q9001-1994 standard
>
> **4.5 DOCUMENT AND DATA CONTROL**
>
> **4.5.1 General**
>
> The supplier shall establish and maintain documented procedures to control all documents and data that relate to the requirements of this American National Standard including, to the extent applicable, documents of external origin such as standards and customer drawings.
>
> NOTE 15 Documents and data can be in the form of any type of media, such as hard copy or electronic media.

What's New?

- **Establishing and maintaining documented procedures to control all documents and data including applicable documents of external origin is a new requirement.**
- Documents can be hard copy or in electronic media.
- The word *data* has been added and refers to numerical information such as product specifications, formulations, process settings, databases, or production schedules.

Guidance

The standard requires the supplier to control all documents and data that are within the scope of the quality system. To implement effective control of documents, the supplier should first identify which are the quality documents and data. The following are often classified as controlled documents.

- Quality manuals
- Quality system–related procedures
- Specifications (raw material, process, manufacturing, product, and package)
- Product formulas/recipes
- Standard operating procedures
- Internal and external laboratory test methods

- Customer-supplied test methods
- Sampling plans
- Industry, national, or international standard test methods when used as work instructions
- Forms
- Work instructions
- ANSI/ISO/ASQC Q9001, Q9002, Q9003, or other applicable quality system standards
- Calibration methods
- Visual standards or templates used for go/no-go inspection

Q9001-1994 standard

4.5.2 Document and data approval and issue

The documents and data shall be reviewed and approved for adequacy by authorized personnel prior to issue. A master list or equivalent document-control procedure identifying the current revision status of documents shall be established and be readily available to preclude the use of invalid and/or obsolete documents.

This control shall ensure that:

a) the pertinent issues of appropriate documents are available at all locations where operations essential to the effective functioning of the quality system are performed;

b) invalid and/or obsolete documents are promptly removed from all points of issue or use, or otherwise assured against unintended use;

c) any obsolete documents retained for legal and/or knowledge-preservation purposes are suitably identified.

What's New?

- Subclause b "otherwise assured against unintended use" adds flexibility to methods used to document control of obsolete documents.
- **Subclause c has been added.**

Guidance

Procedures should define the mechanisms of control, including determining who needs the information and provisions for updating the information. Methods of control may include the use of colored controlled stamps, special paper, or computer control of access, revision, and issue.

The supplier needs to be able to provide the required documentation at the necessary locations. In addition, documents need to be

- Properly reviewed and approved
- Dated, titled, and uniquely identified including revision level
- Removed from service when changed or made obsolete

Archival copies of obsolete documents may be kept if properly identified. Means of identification may include direct marking, storage in a designated area, separate binders from current documents, or separate computer directories.

The supplier should ensure that only the most current version of a controlled document is available at the point of use. This process requires that the supplier know which is the appropriate or most current revision of a document. In larger organizations or where document issuers and users are at different locations, it may be necessary to use some form of acknowledgment of receipt of amendments, revisions, or notices of change to ensure control. Electronic acknowledgment or records are becoming commonplace in networked computer documentation systems.

A document control master list is one way to keep track of controlled documents within each function. Common items listed on a document control master list include functional responsibility, review/approval authority, document title, current date and revision number, and the current holders/location of the document.

There should also be provisions for issuing controlled documents that will not be kept current (for example, when issuing a quality manual to a customer). Controlled documents that are not kept current are often referred to as uncontrolled documents. The supplier should identify these documents as such by marking or stamping "uncontrolled copy" or "for reference only."

> Q9001-1994 standard
>
> **4.5.3 Document and data changes**
>
> Changes to documents and data shall be reviewed and approved by the same functions/organizations that performed the original review and approval, unless specifically designated otherwise. The designated functions/organizations shall have access to pertinent background information upon which to base their review and approval.
>
> Where practicable, the nature of the change shall be identified in the document or the appropriate attachments.

What's New?

- These requirements were separated from those in clause 4.5.2 for improved clarity.

Guidance

Provision for changes to documents and data need to include the information used for the initial creation of the document. Changes to documents are normally made by the person(s) or functions that originally reviewed and approved the proceeding issue of the document, unless specified otherwise. Examples include

- A revision history section of the document
- A description of the change included in a cover letter or attachment
- Vertical change bars in the margin
- Italicizing
- Underlining
- Boldfacing

This change history or notification must remain as part of the document or be attached so that the changes made are known to the holder.

4.6

Purchasing

Introduction

This clause of the standard deals with requirements for how the supplier purchases materials, equipment, and services that affect product quality. The processes of subcontractor selection and evaluation, purchase order processing, and purchased product verification must be carried out according to documented procedures. Remember that the standard is written as requirements the supplier must meet, expressed from the point of view of customers. Therefore, clause 4.6 applies to the entity from whom the supplier purchases products and services—the subcontractor (see Figure 4.6-1).

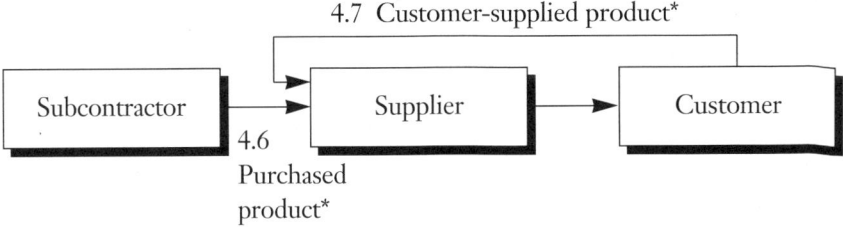

*Products may include equipment, materials, and services.

Figure 4.6-1. Subcontractor–supplier–customer relationship.

Clause 4.6 explicitly refers to purchased product, not to materials provided by the customer, such materials being returned to the customer after processing by the supplier. The latter situation is covered in clause 4.7. The relationship between the two is shown in Figure 4.6-1.

Q9001-1994 standard

4.6 PURCHASING

4.6.1 General

The supplier shall establish and maintain documented procedures to ensure that purchased product (see 3.1) conforms to specified requirements.

What's New?

- Clarifying that purchasing procedures must be documented is new to the standard.

Guidance

Procedures must be prepared for the purchasing of materials, equipment, and services that are deemed critical to the quality of the product provided to the customer. Quality critical or not, all purchases must meet specified requirements. Those that are quality critical will need extra attention. Examples for the CPI might include

- Raw materials
- Utilities, such as steam and process water
- Additives
- Inhibitors
- Solvents
- Catalysts
- Calibration services
- Packaging materials
- Laboratory test equipment and plant instrumentation

- Materials and equipment that come in contact with product
- Transportation services
- Toll processing services
- Storage facilities
- Outside testing services
- Purchased for resale product
- Product exchanges of like product between suppliers

Suppliers should exercise their business judgment in defining which purchased materials and services are defined as critical to quality. Purchased products considered by the chemical industry to be noncritical to product quality might include: office supplies, pumps, valves, piping and other process equipment, maintenance supplies, and general maintenance services. It is the right and the responsibility of the supplier to determine the appropriate levels of quality assurance required for purchased products.

Q9001-1994 standard

4.6.2 Evaluation of subcontractors

The supplier shall:

a) evaluate and select subcontractors on the basis of their ability to meet subcontract requirements including the quality system and any specific quality assurance requirements;

b) define the type and extent of control exercised by the supplier over subcontractors. This shall be dependent upon the type of product, the impact of subcontracted product on the quality of final product, and, where applicable, on the quality audit reports and/or quality records of the previously demonstrated capability and performance of subcontractors;

c) establish and maintain quality records of acceptable subcontractors (see 4.16).

What's New?
- **Factors affecting the controls were clarified to include the impact of the purchased product on the quality of final product.**
- Evaluation in the selection of a subcontractor is added for clarity.

Guidance
Subcontractors should be selected for their ability to consistently meet the supplier's purchased product requirements at a total cost that provides the best value. That is to say that low purchase price alone is not a sufficient criterion by which to select a supplier of quality-critical goods and services.

Evaluation of the subcontractor's ability to consistently meet requirements may be based on evidence such as some of the following:

- On-site assessment of the subcontractor's capability and quality system by the supplier.
- Review and assessment of a subcontractor's prior quality and performance data. This is particularly appropriate in a continuing long-term, satisfactory relationship with a subcontractor.
- Trials or demonstrations in the supplier's laboratories or plant.
- Documented evidence of successful use in similar processes.
- Third-party audits and registration of the subcontractor's quality system to an accepted standard such as Q9001.

The evaluation method selected should ensure that the purchased product consistently meets the requirements of the supplier. Note that audits are not required, but are merely one of many alternative methods for subcontractor evaluation.

The supplier should maintain evaluation data and records of acceptable subcontractors. (*Approved* is a term commonly used in the CPI for *acceptable*.) There should be periodic reviews of the subcontractor's acceptability, performed at intervals consistent with the degree of criticality, complexity, and technical requirements of the product.

The supplier is permitted to determine what constitutes evidence of an acceptable quality system. Assessment against an appropriate standard such as Q9001 or Q9002 may be used to provide the evidence.

Current and historical data may be used to evaluate the subcontractor's capability to meet requirements consistently. It is not a requirement of the standard, but in many cases this is an excellent application for statistical techniques. Statistical evaluation of the data could be used to demonstrate that the subcontractor's process has been maintained in a state of control and that it is capable (C_{pk} or P_{pk}) of meeting specified requirements. If such techniques are employed, clause 4.20.2 requires procedures to ensure their consistent application.

Q9001-1994 standard

4.6.3 Purchasing data

Purchasing documents shall contain data clearly describing the product ordered, including where applicable:

a) the type, class, grade, or other precise identification;

b) the title or other positive identification, and applicable issues of specifications, drawings, process requirements, inspection instructions, and other relevant technical data, including requirements for approval or qualification of product, procedures, process equipment, and personnel;

c) the title, number, and issue of the quality-system standard to be applied.

The supplier shall review and approve purchasing documents for adequacy of the specified requirements prior to release.

What's New?

- There are no changes in this clause.

Guidance

In the CPI, purchasing data are usually communicated to the subcontractor through a contract or purchase order with attendant specifications. Quality requirements are generally contained in a detailed specification. Individual shipments against a purchase order are often covered by a *release*, which refers to the requirements of the original purchase order, rather than repeating them.

Detailed specifications documents should contain the complete technical requirements of the supplier. These may include, for example,

- Chemical composition with target values and limits
- Physical form and composition with size distribution values and limits
- Performance characteristics with values and limits
- Sampling, inspection, and test methods
- Packaging, labeling, transportation, and unloading requirements
- The quality system standard under which the product will be produced
- Quality system and manufacturing process change notification
- Regulatory requirements (for example, FDA, EPA, DoD)
- Product quality data required, such as certificates of analysis or control charts, and method of delivery
- Preshipment sample requirements

The purchasing documents should specify the commercial requirements, for example,

- Identification of product
- Quantity and price
- Delivery mode, date, and location
- Point of ownership transfer

The supplier's purchasing data and documents should be reviewed for technical accuracy and completeness, and approved by authorized personnel before release. Note that the Q9001-required review and approval process is focused on quality requirements, not just financial authorization to expend the funds.

Conferences with subcontractors will help ensure that requirements are clearly defined and understood. The subcontractor should review the purchasing documents and acknowledge acceptance of all specified requirements (in other words, subcontractors should apply clause 4.3 to themselves!).

4.6 Purchasing

> Q9001-1994 standard
>
> **4.6.4 Verification of purchased product**
>
> **4.6.4.1 Supplier verification at subcontractor's premises**
>
> Where the supplier proposes to verify purchased product at the subcontractor's premises, the supplier shall specify verification arrangements and the method of product release in the purchasing documents.
>
> **4.6.4.2 Customer verification of subcontracted product**
>
> Where specified in the contract, the supplier's customer or the customer's representative shall be afforded the right to verify at the subcontractor's premises and the supplier's premises that subcontracted product conforms to specified requirements. Such verification shall not be used by the supplier as evidence of effective control of quality by the subcontractor.
>
> Verification by the customer shall not absolve the supplier of the responsibility to provide acceptable product, nor shall it preclude subsequent rejection by the customer.

What's New?

- Added verification of purchased product by the supplier at the subcontractor's premises is new to this clause.

Guidance

This part of Q9001 is often misunderstood or misinterpreted. In the CPI, subclause 4.6.4 is seldom invoked. The *verification* referred to in clause 4.6.4 should not be confused with *receiving inspection* in clause 4.10.2. Figure 4.6-2 shows where the three possible verifications occur, as well as the receiving inspection.

Subclause 4.6.4.1 refers to a situation in which the supplier desires to check and approve or accept the product while it is still at the subcontractor's premises. This often happens for very large and expensive process equipment, such as compressors, but rarely happens for the type of quality-critical materials and services described earlier in this chapter.

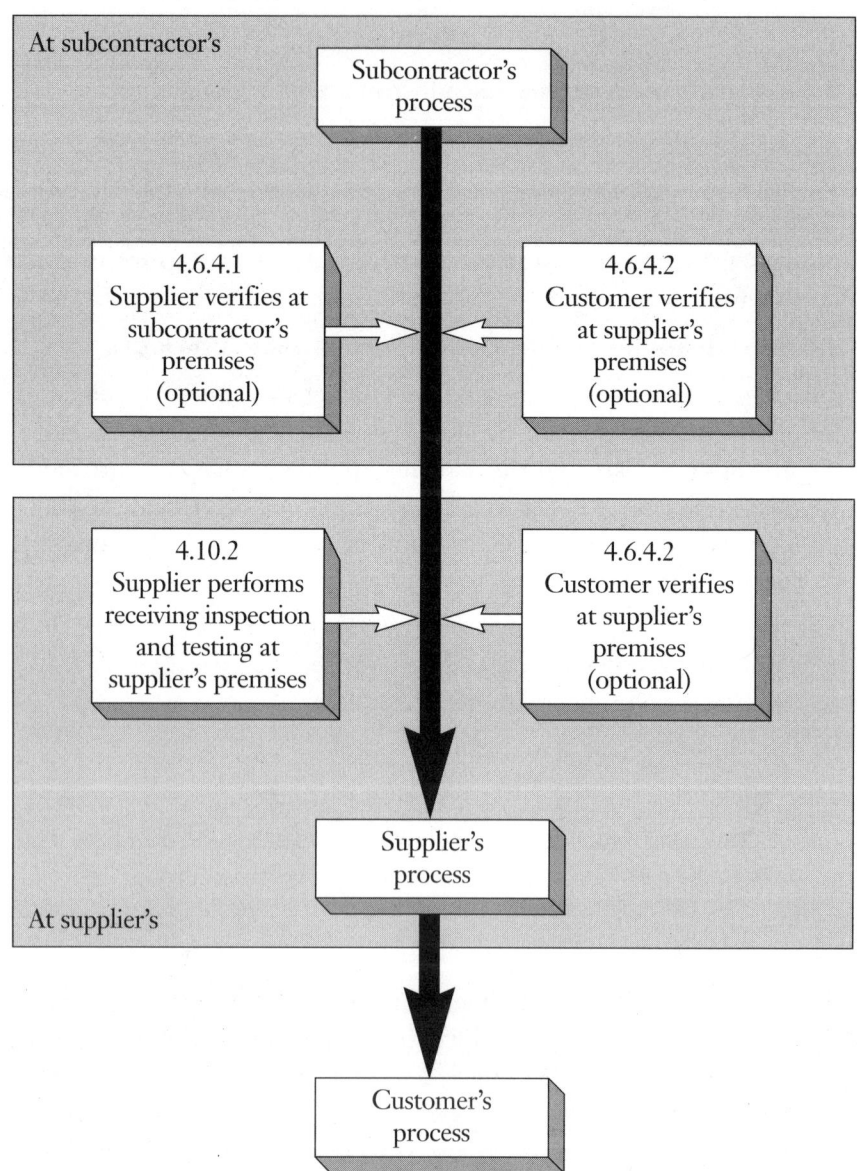

Figure 4.6-2. Product verification contrasted with receiving inspection.

If it is a requirement, then the supplier must ensure that the purchase order or contract gives the right to make such a verification. Note that the verification in clause 4.6.4.1 does not involve the customer in any way.

The second subclause does involve the customer. In some situations, the customer (or a third-party inspector hired by the customer) may wish to make a similar verification, either at the subcontractor's or the supplier's premises. If this requirement is specified in the contract between the customer and supplier, then the supplier is responsible for transferring this requirement to the subcontractor in the purchasing documents.

Subclause 4.6.2b requires the supplier to maintain control over the subcontractor. In the event the customer elects to perform independent verification, this does not let the supplier off the hook from a responsibility to control the subcontractor. Similarly, verification by the customer of purchased product does not change the fundamental responsibility of the supplier to provide acceptable product to the customer. For example, if the customer verifies and accepts the raw material, the customer still retains the right to reject the finished product from the supplier's process.

Clause 4.6, Purchasing, is not included in Q9003.

4.7

Control of Customer-Supplied Product

Introduction

This clause of the standard covers requirements for control of product supplied by the customer.

> Q9001-1994 standard
>
> **4.7 CONTROL OF CUSTOMER-SUPPLIED PRODUCT**
>
> The supplier shall establish and maintain documented procedures for the control of verification, storage, and maintenance of customer-supplied product provided for incorporation into the supplies or for related activities. Any such product that is lost, damaged, or is otherwise unsuitable for use shall be recorded and reported to the customer (see 4.16).
>
> Verification by the supplier does not absolve the customer of the responsibility to provide acceptable product.

What's New?
- Procedures must be documented.

Guidance

Customer-supplied product is product owned by the customer and furnished to the supplier for use in meeting the requirements of the contract (see Figure 4.6-1). The supplier will need to develop and install systems to control receipt, verification, identification, condition, and traceability for products or related materials supplied by the customer. The documented procedures will include maintaining records and reporting to the customer any customer-supplied product that is lost, damaged, or becomes unsuitable for use. Suppliers should treat customer-supplied product as diligently as purchased product.

Customer-supplied product may be materials to be incorporated into the product; materials or equipment to be used in manufacturing, testing, or packaging of the product; or services. In the CPI, this may include raw materials, additives, blend components, special manufacturing equipment, test equipment, tooling, containers, packaging supplies, labels, or other packaging materials. Services may include testing, inspections, packaging, or transportation services.

This clause also applies to conversion or toll manufacturing arrangements between the customer and supplier where the customer provides materials or services.

Depending on the terms of the contract, the following may be important.

- The customer is responsible for providing acceptable materials or services.
- The supplier must verify upon receipt: identity, quantity, quality testing or inspection requirements, and condition of the product.
- The supplier accepts responsibility for maintaining condition, traceability, and accountability for the material until used or returned.

4.8

Product Identification and Traceability

Introduction

This clause of the standard covers requirements for identification and traceability of product.

> Q9001-1994 standard
> **4.8 PRODUCT IDENTIFICATION AND TRACEABILITY**
>
> Where appropriate, the supplier shall establish and maintain documented procedures for identifying the product by suitable means from receipt and during all stages of production, delivery, and installation.
>
> Where and to the extent that traceability is a specified requirement, the supplier shall establish and maintain documented procedures for unique identification of individual product or batches. This identification shall be recorded (see 4.16).

What's New?

- The standard provides more flexibility for means of identifying product.
- This clause now clarifies that procedures must be documented.

Guidance

Product *identification* provides the means of distinguishing one product from another. This includes similar products, such as those constituting multiple grades within a product line, as well as like products manufactured at different times or locations. Identification ensures that personnel can conclusively determine which of several products or grades of product they are concerned with.

Product *traceability* provides a record of a product's manufacturing history, including the identification of raw materials, intermediates, and equipment used in its production.

A fundamental requisite to either function is a working definition of what constitutes a batch or lot of raw materials, intermediates, and finished products.

Traceability provides a means of tracking product so that if a nonconformity or other problem is discovered after the product has passed final inspection and testing, all affected customers can be promptly notified. Traceability also facilitates cause-and-effect analysis, making it easier to understand the process and make corrections and improvements. For example, this can be helpful if a process shift can be traced to a change in raw materials. Concepts of traceability are shown in Figure 4.8-1.

It is often difficult to designate or identify precise lots or batches from a continuous process. Even in the case of a batch process, the batch identity is often difficult to maintain due to downstream blending. Identification and traceability of some bulk products may only be accomplished through recording of production times, flow rates, and location and unit configuration. Use of tags or other discrete identifiers may be impractical or impossible.

The product identification system must be documented. Product identification may be addressed in the following manner.

- Each product should be uniquely identifiable during the manufacturing, storage, delivery, and installation process. In the CPI this often means keeping time-line records, especially where reactions or blending occur.
- Each product should be uniquely identified and have applicable product and manufacturing specifications and/or technical data

4.8 Product Identification and Traceability

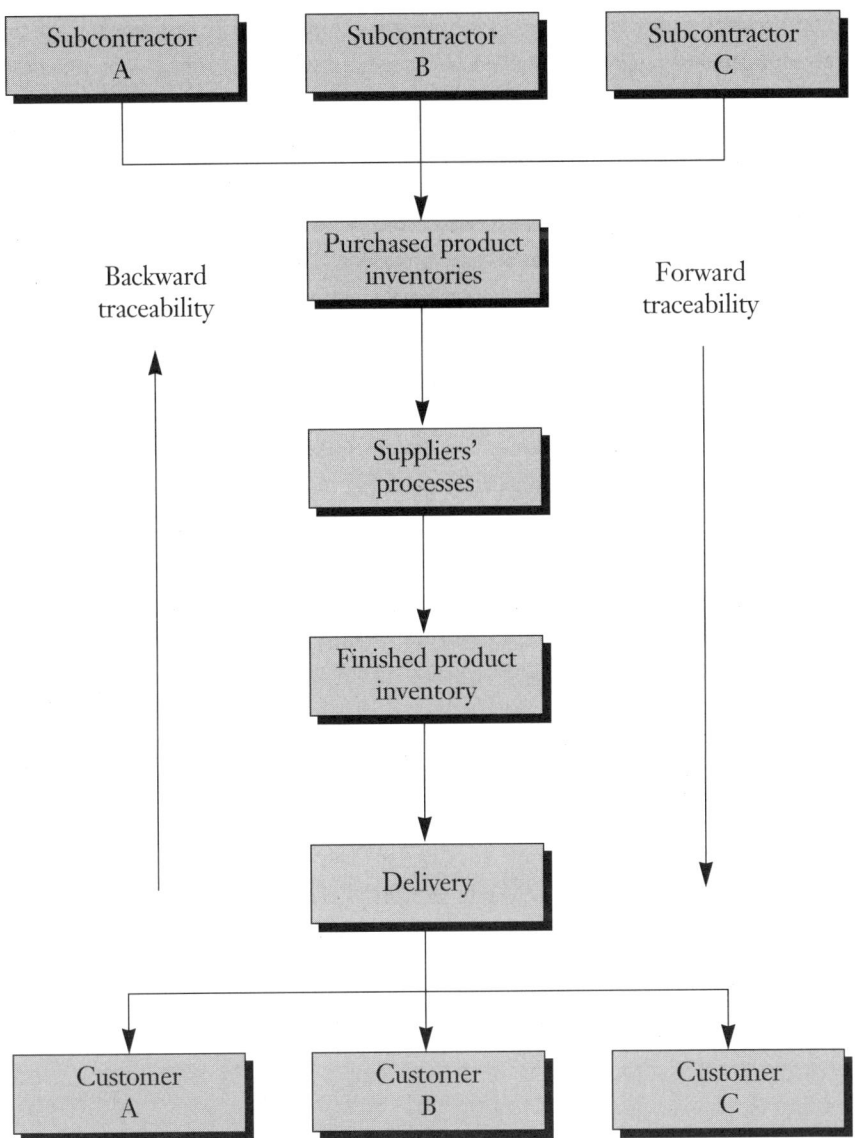

Figure 4.8-1. Traceability.

sheets that provide sufficient information to distinguish one product from another.
- Unique product identification should be maintained throughout the manufacturing and the handling, packing, storage, and delivery operations.

The standard only requires traceability if the customer specifies it as a requirement. In regulated markets, such as FDA, however, the need for full traceability should be an assumed requirement. The product traceability system should be documented and maintained. Product traceability may be addressed in the following manner.

- Batches or lots should have unique identification codes.
- Product traceability records should be retained.
- Product traceability data may include batch numbers of raw materials, identification of process equipment used, production and laboratory data generated during the manufacturing process, records of product disposition, and applicable customer information.
- Providing traceability trails is always a good idea for possible problem-solving efforts.
- Traceability should be possible both from the raw materials to the finished product and from the finished product back to the raw materials.

Product identification and traceability records may form the basis for application of various statistical methods either for process improvement or for corrective and preventive actions.

Q9003 does not include requirements for product identification.

4.9

Process Control

Introduction

This clause of the standard defines the requirements for a system to manage and control production operations that affect quality. The objective is to achieve consistent, predictable production operations in conformance with requirements. In the CPI, *process control* usually refers specifically to a system (often computerized) of sensors, and analyzers and controllers with feedback loops. The standard, however, uses the term in a broader sense to encompass all of the production, installation, and servicing operations.

> Q9001-1994 standard
>
> **4.9 PROCESS CONTROL**
>
> The supplier shall identify and plan the production, installation, and servicing processes which directly affect quality and shall ensure that these processes are carried out under controlled conditions. Controlled conditions shall include the following:
>
> a) documented procedures defining the manner of production, installation, and servicing, where the absence of such procedures could adversely affect quality;

What's New?
- **Inclusion of servicing processes is new.**
- There is now a requirement for documented procedures when quality could adversely be affected by their absence.

Guidance

Establishing an effective process control system requires knowledge of the process and of the relationship between product characteristics and the key process variables. Process knowledge and determination of these relationships begins in research and continues throughout the product life cycle.

The process control system should provide written procedures that may include

- Process recipes, work orders, and batch sheets
- Start-up, shutdown, and order change procedures
- Standard operating procedures
- Flowcharts
- Equipment and maintenance requirements
- Specific sampling requirements
- Safety and environmental requirements
- Target values and/or limit requirements for process variables
- Target values and/or limit requirements for product characteristics
- Control response when limits are violated
- The handling requirements needed to preserve product quality
- The process variable and product measurements required
- Whom to contact concerning changes to the operation

Written procedures are not required for every activity, only for those where training and education by themselves are not sufficient (see clause 4.18). Documented procedures are especially important where their absence could adversely affect the ability to meet contract requirements (see clause 4.3). Be aware that overdocumentation may limit the flexibility necessary to complete assigned tasks, thus not adding value.

Production planning and scheduling are normally included as process control procedures. In some processes, special equipment may be necessary to successfully produce the product. If so, scheduling would consider these special equipment requirements when creating the production plan or schedule.

Q9001-1994 standard

4.9 PROCESS CONTROL (continued)

Controlled conditions shall include the following:

b) use of suitable production, installation, and servicing equipment, and a suitable working environment;

c) compliance with reference standards/codes, quality plans, and/or documented procedures;

What's New?

- Servicing equipment is now mentioned.

Guidance

Selection of equipment or processes should include

- The ability to operate under required conditions.
- Provision of the proper working environment and controlling it. This often includes housekeeping, lighting, noise, climate control, and safety hazards.

Reference standards and codes could include items such as OSHA, ASTM, GMP, Food Chemical Codex, API, ASME, USDA, and so on.

Q9001-1994 standard

4.9 PROCESS CONTROL (continued)

Controlled conditions shall include the following:

d) monitoring and control of suitable process parameters and product characteristics;

e) the approval of processes and equipment, as appropriate;

> f) criteria for workmanship, which shall be stipulated in the clearest practical manner (e.g., written standards, representative samples, or illustrations);
>
> g) suitable maintenance of equipment to ensure continuing process capability.

What's New?
- **Consideration of maintenance of equipment is now a requirement.**

Guidance
Control strategies are needed for each of the key process variables and key product characteristics, which

- Specify the actions to be taken to keep key process variables and product characteristics within requirements
- Indicate where control of variability is necessary
- Describe appropriate statistical tools to be used (Shewhart control charts are often useful here.)

Other clauses that relate strongly to this one include

- Receiving inspection (clause 4.10.2)
- In-process inspection (clause 4.10.3)
- Quality planning (clause 4.2.3)
- Inspection, measuring, and test equipment (clause 4.11)
- Statistical techniques (clause 4.20)

Criteria for workmanship are needed that allow operating personnel to make decisions concerning the acceptability of their work. In the CPI, the appearance of a product is often the only aspect that an operator can judge firsthand. Verification of product quality by analytical means often takes time because of the location of analytical tools and the time to obtain results. Thus, clear descriptions and/or samples of acceptable and unacceptable appearance should be provided to the operators. Criteria can be expressed in words and by examples. The criteria should clearly describe both acceptable and unacceptable product where possible.

Some examples of physical descriptions of product appearance are
- Fine brown powder free of foreign contaminants
- Green clear liquid
- Milk-white uniform emulsion
- Uniform, free flowing mixture of green and tan spheres

Descriptions or examples might also be provided for
- Finished package appearance
- Attributes of damaged, contaminated, or deformed products
- Labeling of products or packages

Item g in clause 4.9 covers maintenance of process equipment, not test equipment, as needed to continue to meet quality needs. The supplier should define *suitable maintenance* to meet its business needs. Process capability, as used here, does not necessarily refer to statistical capability, but rather the ability to continue to perform the tasks needed to meet agreed upon requirements. A typical CPI preventive/predictive maintenance program easily exceeds the requirement of item g.

Q9001-1994 standard

4.9 PROCESS CONTROL (continued)

Where the results of processes cannot be fully verified by subsequent inspection and testing of the product and where, for example, processing deficiencies may become apparent only after the product is in use, the processes shall be carried out by qualified operators and/or shall require continuous monitoring and control of process parameters to ensure that the specified requirements are met.

The requirements for any qualification of process operations, including associated equipment and personnel (see 4.18), shall be specified.

NOTE 16 Such processes requiring prequalification of their process capability are frequently referred to as special processes.

Records shall be maintained for qualified processes, equipment, and personnel, as appropriate (see 4.16).

What's New?

- The requirement pertaining to special processes has been moved from a stand-alone subclause to the main body of the clause.
- Requirements for qualification of process operations, equipment, and personnel must be specified.

Guidance

The results or outcomes of most CPI processes can only be measured downstream of the process. Good process records should be kept. There should be a system for qualification of quality sensitive equipment, processes, operators, and technicians wherever quality may be impacted. Verification of the capability of special processes should address

- The accuracy and variability of equipment used to make or measure product, including settings and adjustments
- The skill, capability, and knowledge of operators to meet quality requirements
- Special environments, time, temperature, or other factors affecting quality
- The frequency of testing, based on a study of the stability of the process for which process limits are defined

Q9003 does not include clause 4.9, Process Control.

4.10

Inspection and Testing

Introduction

This clause of the standard covers requirements for inspection and testing of incoming products, in-process materials, and final products, whether measured in a laboratory or on-line.

Sampling plans are essential elements of inspection and testing. These plans should consider

- Sampling methodology
- Whether or not the test is destructive
- Process capability
- Test capability
- Sample stability
- Measurement error in proportion to total variability
- Time to complete the test relative to process cycle times
- Time for the process to stabilize following an upset or intentional change
- Customer or statutory requirements
- Cost of failure to detect a nonconformance
- Cost of test

- Uniformity of sample
- Ability of sample to represent the product

> **Q9001-1994 standard**
>
> **4.10 INSPECTION AND TESTING**
>
> **4.10.1 General**
>
> The supplier shall establish and maintain documented procedures for inspection and testing activities in order to verify that the specified requirements for the product are met. The required inspection and testing, and the records to be established, shall be detailed in the quality plan or documented procedures.
>
> **4.10.2 Receiving inspection and testing**
>
> **4.10.2.1** The supplier shall ensure that incoming product is not used or processed (except in the circumstances described in 4.10.2.3) until it has been inspected or otherwise verified as conforming to specified requirements. Verification of the specified requirements shall be in accordance with the quality plan and/or documented procedures.

What's New?

- The standard now requires the supplier to clarify the requirements for all inspection and text processes.

Guidance

Clause 4.10.2 applies to both purchased products and customer-supplied products. Receiving inspection includes verifying that subcontractors have fulfilled their contractual obligations for quality and that procured items or substances entering suppliers' facilities meet specified requirements. This verification applies to both service and product aspects of incoming material. At the time of receiving inspection, positive identification of raw materials may be made in order to provide traceability (see clause 4.8).

The method used to ensure the quality of purchased materials and services received by the supplier depends on the importance of the item to product or process quality, the state of control (process or product), past performance of the subcontractor, information available from the subcontractor, and impact on costs (see clause 4.6).

Packaged materials should be segregated to avoid use before acceptance. This segregation may be achieved by physical or nonphysical means. Bulk materials require that issues of commingling, identification, and traceability be addressed and documented. The supplier should maintain sufficient control and traceability, even if pipeline shipments or large tanks are involved.

Introduction of new bulk materials into the inventory of existing materials raises the potential for cross-contamination. In some cases (for example, pipeline shipments), raw materials proceed directly from the subcontractor's process without going into inventory and are immediately consumed in the supplier's process. Such cases require a high level of confidence in the subcontractor's quality system. In these instances, receiving inspection may be done by on-line analyzers or analysis of control charts of critical raw material parameters.

Q9001-1994 standard

4.10.2.2 In determining the amount and nature of receiving inspection, consideration shall be given to the amount of control exercised at the subcontractor's premises and the recorded evidence of conformance provided.

What's New?

- A note in the earlier standard is now a requirement.

Guidance

This element does not imply that incoming items must be inspected and tested by the supplier. Receiving verification of other specifications can be limited to checking objective evidence provided by subcontractors. The basis for verification (for example, certificates of analysis) must be documented in a procedure or quality plan.

The supplier's procedures for receiving inspection should include the means for verifying that shipments are complete, properly identified, undamaged, and accompanied by supporting documentation if required (for example, test reports or control charts).

Procedures should also specify corrective actions to follow in the event of nonconformance. Analysis of past receiving inspection data can influence the supplier's decisions regarding the need to reassess the subcontractor's capabilities.

The nature and extent of receiving inspection should be designed to take into account the levels of process control and finished product testing that are performed by the subcontractor. Also a factor is the level of test result detail provided by the subcontractor.

Incoming product acceptance procedures should be developed, taking into consideration process requirements and subcontractor's process capability. The goal is to minimize or eliminate the need for formal incoming lot acceptance and to rely on the subcontractor to supply materials and services that continually meet requirements. Supporting documentation may be required in the form of certification, data sharing, or statistical evidence. Minimal inspection or testing may still be required for identification, to detect changes that occur during shipment, or for safety reasons.

Q9001-1994 standard

4.10.2.3 Where incoming product is released for urgent production purposes prior to verification, it shall be positively identified and recorded (see 4.16) in order to permit immediate recall and replacement in the event of nonconformity to specified requirements.

What's New?

- This clause has been clarified and the phrase "prior to verification" has been added.

Guidance

This clause of the standard covers the situation in which material is used before incoming verification has been completed. In this case, the standard requires total traceability. Acceptance and use of incoming product subject to recall should be strongly discouraged as a matter of good quality management practice. Items should be released only if

- An objective evaluation of quality status and resolution of any nonconformity can still be implemented.
- Correction of nonconformity cannot compromise the quality of adjacent, attached, incorporated items, or materials.

To achieve the control required, acceptance of bulk raw materials without appropriate receiving inspection should be avoided. Once product has been pumped into tanks or blown into silos, its positive identification is lost through mixing with existing inventory. For packaged products, the subcontractor's batch numbers may provide adequate positive identification.

Q9001-1994 standard

4.10.3 In-process inspection and testing

The supplier shall:

a) inspect and test the product as required by the quality plan and/or documented procedures;

b) hold product until the required inspection and tests have been completed or necessary reports have been received and verified, except when product is released under positive-recall procedures (see 4.10.2.3). Release under positive-recall procedures shall not preclude the activities outlined in 4.10.3a.

What's New?

- The process monitoring requirement subclause is deleted, which is covered in clause 4.9.
- The identification of nonconforming product requirement is also deleted since it adequately covered in clause 4.13.1.

Guidance

This clause applies to all tests performed after incoming inspection and before final inspection. Measurements that are critical to quality must be identified and controlled as part of the quality management system. The test results are often used both to control the process and to verify conformance to requirements. Monitoring of process parameters is addressed in clause 4.9d.

Inspections or tests should be considered at appropriate points in the process to verify conformity. Location and frequency will depend on the importance of the characteristics and ease of verification at the stage of production. Verification should be made as close as possible to the point where the feature or characteristic is first measurable.

In-process inspection and testing may include

- Automatic analysis or inspection (for example, material composition by on-line gas chromatographs, infrared scanners for moisture content)
- Off-line chemical and physical analyses (for example, composition of sample)
- Designated physical inspection stations within the process (for example, visual inspection of color)

Statistical process control methodology (see clause 4.20), applied in process, will often provide early warning of problems before nonconformities occur.

The point of control and the acceptable ranges should be defined for each of the in-process measurements. In general, product should be held until the required verifications have been completed. Procedures for positive recall apply to in-process product as well as raw materials. Nonconforming product needs to be identified and controlled (see clause 4.13).

Documented procedures should indicate the actions to be followed when values for monitored parameters fall outside the acceptable range (see clause 4.9).

Q9001-1994 standard

4.10.4 Final inspection and testing

The supplier shall carry out all final inspection and testing in accordance with the quality plan and/or documented procedures to complete the evidence of conformance of the finished product to the specified requirements.

> The quality plan and/or documented procedures for final inspection and testing shall require that all specified inspection and tests, including those specified either on receipt of product or in-process, have been carried out and that the results meet specified requirements.
>
> No product shall be dispatched until all the activities specified in the quality plan and/or documented procedures have been satisfactorily completed and the associated data and documentation are available and authorized.

What's New?

- These paragraphs were rearranged without substantial changes.

Guidance

The quality plan or the quality procedures should define the required final inspections and tests. The requirements of this section apply to finished product and service before dispatch. *Dispatch* needs to be carefully defined and the definition should include factors such as mode of transportation, who owns the product while in transit, and where the title change takes place. This is the point in the quality assurance system where the supplier generates evidence that the finished product meets specified requirements.

Final inspection is defined as the activities (examination, inspection, measurement, or test) upon which the release of product or service with respect to specified characteristics is based. Suitable procedures should be established so that each unit or lot of product or service is not released until the required inspections and tests show that the product or service meets specified requirements. Finished product verification has these important roles.

- To ensure that raw material and in-process testing was completed
- To confirm predictions based on process parameters
- To guide longer-term process adjustments
- To provide the basis for product acceptance or rejection
- To provide data for statistical analysis of process and product performance

To augment inspections and test made during production, at least two forms of final verification of finished product are available. Either of the following may be used, as appropriate.

- Final inspections or tests, to ensure that items or lots produced have met performance and other quality requirements. Reference should be made to the purchase order to verify that product to be shipped agrees in type and quantity. Examples include 100-percent inspection, lot sampling, and continuous sampling.
- Prediction of conformance based on process knowledge and test results.

Release inspection and product quality auditing may provide feedback for corrective action on product and process.

The quality plans, documented procedures, or contracts should clearly specify if there are any circumstances under which product may be released before completion of final inspection. Examples would include pipeline transfers, immediate mobilization of vehicles to avoid demurrage, and long cycle-time testing.

Q9001-1994 standard

4.10.5 Inspection and test records

The supplier shall establish and maintain records which provide evidence that the product has been inspected and/or tested. These records shall show clearly whether the product has passed or failed the inspections and/or tests according to defined acceptance criteria. Where the product fails to pass any inspection and/or test, the procedures for control of nonconforming product shall apply (see 4.13).

Records shall identify the inspection authority responsible for the release of product (see 4.16).

What's New?

- The requirement for identification of release authority was moved here from clause 4.12.

Guidance

Record-keeping requirements should be well-defined and reviewed periodically. The records should show whether product passed or failed the required test. A specific reference to clause 4.13 is given when product is found to be nonconforming. Responsibility for release of conforming product must be assigned and documented. Retention of inspection and test records must be documented and maintained.

Records are needed to show that all required inspections have been made on all products including raw materials, and in-process and final products. Inspection authority is the person responsible for verifying that the product meets requirements and can be transferred to the next operation.

In circumstances where in-process inspection and testing are achieved by monitoring in-process instrumentation, the records for this part of the inspection should also be kept. If certificates of analysis were used during receiving inspection procedures, then these certificates will form part of the inspection and test records.

Q9003 does not include receiving and in-process inspection and testing.

4.11

Control of Inspection, Measuring, and Test Equipment

Introduction

This clause of the standard covers requirements for inspection, measuring, and test equipment. It applies to equipment used in meeting the requirements for receiving, in-process, and final inspection and testing (see clause 4.10). It is helpful to approach this element from the perspective that each measurement system is a process involving materials, equipment, procedures, and people. In the CPI this equipment consists of

- Laboratory equipment
- On-line analyzers
- Process instrumentation
- Research and development equipment (if Q9001)

Any of these that are used to verify conformance with specified requirements must be calibrated and maintained in accordance with this clause. Equipment that is not used to verify conformance with specified requirements may need to be maintained in accordance with subclause 4.9g.

> Q9001-1994 standard
>
> **4.11 CONTROL OF INSPECTION, MEASURING, AND TEST EQUIPMENT**
>
> **4.11.1 General**
>
> The supplier shall establish and maintain documented procedures to control, calibrate, and maintain inspection, measuring, and test equipment (including test software) used by the supplier to demonstrate the conformance of product to the specified requirements. Inspection, measuring, and test equipment shall be used in a manner which ensures that the measurement uncertainty is known and is consistent with the required measurement capability.
>
> Where test software or comparative references such as test hardware are used as suitable forms of inspection, they shall be checked to prove that they are capable of verifying the acceptability of product, prior to release for use during production, installation, or servicing, and shall be rechecked at prescribed intervals. The supplier shall establish the extent and frequency of such checks and shall maintain records as evidence of control (see 4.16).
>
> Where the availability of technical data pertaining to the measurement equipment is a specified requirement, such data shall be made available, when required by the customer or customer's representative, for verification that the measuring equipment is functionally adequate.
>
> NOTE 17 For the purposes of this American National Standard, the term "measuring equipment" includes measurement devices.

What's New?

- Documented procedures are now required.
- Servicing has been added.
- The term *measuring equipment* has been defined.

Guidance

Sufficient control should be maintained over all measurement systems used to provide confidence in any decisions or actions based on measurement data. Control should be exercised over gauges, instruments, sensors, special test equipment, and related computer software. Where computer software is used as part of the measurement system, it is necessary to validate the performance of the software before it is used to release material for use or sale. In addition, process instrumentation that can affect the specified characteristics of a product should be suitably controlled.

For both product and service measurement systems, statistical methods are valuable tools for achieving and demonstrating conformity to requirements. In particular, statistical methods are preferred tools in fulfilling the overall requirement that "equipment shall be used in a manner which ensures that measurement uncertainty is known and is consistent with the required measurement capability." These methods may also be used to monitor and maintain critical measurements systems in a state of statistical control.

Records and data from measurement system design, development, and control should be kept. The customer or customer's representative may request and review this data to verify the adequacy of the supplier's measurement systems.

The following subclauses spell out in detail what is to be implemented in the quality system for measuring equipment.

Q9001-1994 standard

4.11.2 Control procedure

The supplier shall:

a) determine the measurements to be made and the accuracy required, and select the appropriate inspection, measuring, and test equipment that is capable of the necessary accuracy and precision;

What's New?

- Accuracy and precision requirements were moved to this subclause for clarity.

Guidance

The supplier will need to identify all measurements required to demonstrate that the product is in conformance with requirements. This will include measurements of raw materials, in-process goods, and finished product. In general terms, wherever inspection, measuring, or test equipment provides data required by the quality system, then the equipment should be identified, controlled, calibrated, and maintained in accordance with the requirements of this clause.

The focus in this clause is on the equipment used to control and/or verify product quality. Plant instrumentation and test equipment provided for purposes such as safety, environmental control, energy consumption, or material consumption may remain outside the quality system. Many organizations find it to be good practice to include most instruments in the system, especially in situations where instruments not normally used within the quality system are occasionally used for quality systems purposes, for backup, or for other reasons.

For each measurement, test equipment must be specified and selected that will provide the appropriate accuracy, precision, robustness, and reliability under actual conditions of service.

Q9001-1994 standard

4.11.2 Control procedure (continued)

The supplier shall:

b) identify all inspection, measuring, and test equipment that can affect product quality, and calibrate and adjust them at prescribed intervals, or prior to use, against certified equipment having a known valid relationship to internationally or nationally recognized standards. Where no such standards exist, the basis used for calibration shall be documented;

What's New?

- The clause includes an added reference to international standards.

Guidance

The calibration of inspection, measuring, and test equipment should include the following:

- Initial checking of calibration prior to use, verifying conformance to the required accuracy and precision. The software and procedures controlling automatic test equipment should also be verified.
- Periodic scheduled checks of the measurement equipment. When outside of acceptance criteria, recalibration, adjustment, or repair must be done to reestablish the required precision and accuracy in use. Recalibration should generally be done only when checks indicate the measurement equipment is statistically out of control. Records of each recalibration and adjustment must be maintained. Excessive recalibration can increase total variability.
- Traceability of calibrants to national or international standards, if they exist. Where such recognized reference standards do not exist, internal standards may be used. The basis for selection and use of these internal standards must be documented. Preparation and testing of these internal standards should be in accord with documented and approved procedures.

Guidance on the general requirements for assuring the quality of calibration may be found in ISO 10012 Part 1 and for measurement assurance in ISO/CD 10012 Part 2.

The use of a primary reference material or calibrant to check accuracy (lack of bias) often validates only part of a given measurement process. The process industry frequently uses internal reference materials, together with statistical methods, to validate the complete measurement process.

> Q9001-1994 standard
>
> **4.11.2 Control procedure (continued)**
>
> The supplier shall:
>
> c) define the process employed for the calibration of inspection, measuring, and test equipment, including details of equipment type, unique identification, location, frequency of checks, check method, acceptance criteria, and the action to be taken when results are unsatisfactory;

What's New?

- The process for calibration must be defined.

Guidance

The supplier should consider the following guidance in developing and documenting procedures.

- Calibration procedures must be documented, approved, maintained, and controlled as a part of the quality system.
- Supplier must identify detail of equipment type, identification, and location.
- Supplier must define frequency, method acceptance critical, and the action to be taken.
- The acceptance criteria should be the precision and accuracy required for the most stringent test for which that equipment is used.
- Where measurement equipment is determined to be out of control or outside acceptance limits, corrective action is necessary (see clause 4.14.2). Review of statistical control records is often a necessary and useful step in identifying when and if corrective actions are needed. If statistical records show the measurement process to be out of control (in other words, a special cause exists), the user should remove the cause prior to recalibration.
- The time interval between calibration checks and maintenance must be reasonable for the requirement; the supplier determines

4.11 Control of Inspection, Measuring, and Test Equipment

this based on experience and knowledge of how the equipment is used. The equipment and, where appropriate, materials used in testing must be checked, calibrated, and maintained according to written procedures.

Manufacturers of standard measuring gauges or instruments will specify and, often, supply certification of the precision and accuracy of their equipment as shipped. These specifications or certifications of capability should be compared to the requirements of the process, contract, quality system, or test methods. Verification of the device's capability against the manufacturer's certification or specification is recommended. This information should be included in the documentation of the quality system for inspection, measuring, and test equipment.

In the process industry, complex measuring equipment and procedures are common. Development of special measurements systems should include determinations of precision and accuracy. Consider including the customer's laboratory in studies of test methods for finished products. These studies should be conducted using accepted procedures such as round-robin testing.

In the CPI, subcontractors often provide calibration services. In these instances, the supplier is not required to maintain a copy of the vendor's calibration procedure; however, purchasing documentation should clearly identify the calibration requirements the subcontractor is expected to fulfill.

Evaluation of any measurement system's capability should include studies of the variation due to sampling. In the CPI, variance due to the sampling procedures is often highly significant. Control of sampling procedures is a necessary part of measurement equipment control.

Q9001-1994 standard

4.11.2 Control procedure (continued)

The supplier shall:

d) identify inspection, measuring, and test equipment with a suitable indicator or approved identification record to show the calibration status;

What's New?

- There is no change in this subclause.

Guidance

A widely used method for compliance with clause 4.11.2d is the physical tagging of each and every piece of inspection, measuring, or test equipment. The tag may provide device identification, the current status of its calibration, the identification of the person who performed the calibration, and the next calibration date.

In the CPI, where hundreds of measuring devices are used in a production process, practical alternatives may be used, such as computer-based records with provisions for verification of calibration status. The user must be able to demonstrate that the system effectively prevents the use of results from a critical inspection, measuring, or test device when the calibration check is overdue.

For each measurement equipment included in the scope of this requirement, it is necessary to identify both equipment and materials used to make the measurements. The particular materials (for example, standard analytical solutions and buffer solutions) should be identified by a tag number, label, or other suitable means that meets safety requirements and indicates the expiration date of the material.

Q9001-1994 standard

4.11.2 Control procedure (continued)

The supplier shall:

e) maintain calibration records for inspection, measuring, and test equipment (see 4.16);

What's New?

- There is no change.

Guidance

In addition to the calibration status, records for each piece of inspection, measuring, or test equipment should include all of the data required in

4.11 Control of Inspection, Measuring, and Test Equipment

clause 4.11.2e. These records must also be maintained by the supplier for equipment calibrated by subcontractors.

Records of routine maintenance and verification of the measurement equipment precision and accuracy during production may include control charting of data obtained using reference or standard samples.

Q9001-1994 standard

4.11.2 Control procedure (continued)

The supplier shall:

f) assess and document the validity of previous inspection and test results when inspection, measuring, and test equipment is found to be out of calibration;

What's New?

- There is no change.

Guidance

It is important to look back at prior records to try to understand reasons for the equipment to have changed in performance.

When a measurement system is found to be out of calibration or out of statistical control, this subclause requires an assessment of previous product measurements obtained with the measurement equipment. Product produced while measurements were in error may need to be quarantined and require retesting to verify conformance to requirements. Action may have to include analysis of retained samples, quarantine product recall, or customer notification. Records must be maintained of the results of measurement verification.

Q9001-1994 standard

4.11.2 Control procedure (continued)

The supplier shall:

g) ensure that the environmental conditions are suitable for the calibrations, inspections, measurements, and tests being carried out;

> h) ensure that the handling, preservation, and storage of inspection, measuring, and test equipment is such that the accuracy and fitness for use are maintained;
>
> i) safeguard inspection, measuring, and test facilities, including both test hardware and test software, from adjustments which would invalidate the calibration setting.
>
> NOTE 18 The metrological confirmation system for measuring equipment given in ISO 10012 may be used for guidance.

What's New?

- Reference to ISO 10012 has been added.

Guidance

These sections of the standard contain requirements for ensuring that the capability of all inspection, measuring, and test equipment is protected from damage or inadvertent adjustments. Appropriate protective devices, shielding, and work instructions should be incorporated into the quality system to protect this equipment. The environmental conditions in which the measurement equipment is used should be appropriately specified and maintained.

The requirement relating to test hardware or software will apply to such things as

- Molds or dies used to prepare samples for testing
- Standard color plaques
- Reference samples used to evaluate appearance, fragrance, and other factors
- Software used for spectrum analysis and so on
- Automatic titrators and gas chromatographic equipment

Note 18 suggests that ISO 10012 may be used for guidance, however, it is not a requirement.

4.12

Inspection and Test Status

Introduction

This clause of the standard provides supplementary requirements for product identification and traceability. It refers specifically to the status of product regarding the results of inspections or tests that are performed on the product. Included is the status of product from receipt of raw materials through finished product until ownership is transferred to the customer.

Q9001-1994 standard

4.12 INSPECTION AND TEST STATUS

The inspection and test status of product shall be identified by suitable means, which indicate the conformance or nonconformance of product with regard to inspection and tests performed. The identification of inspection and test status shall be maintained, as defined in the quality plan and/or documented procedures, throughout production, installation, and servicing of the product to ensure that only product that has passed the required inspections and tests [or released under an authorized concession (see 4.13.2)] is dispatched, used, or installed.

What's New?

- **Identification and test status must be maintained as defined in quality plan or documented procedures.**
- References to authorized tags, stamps, labels, and so on have been deleted and replaced by suitable means for identifying the status.

Guidance

These requirements apply to the inspection and test status of purchased products, customer-supplied products, in-process materials, and finished products. The status of any material in storage or in-process, with respect to any test required by the quality plan, should be known and available. The test status of any material is generally either not yet known, passed (conforming), or failed (nonconforming).

Direct labeling of a material's test status is often unsuitable for chemical products (see clause 4.8). Records of test results from the control laboratory, production logs, documentation of bulk shipments, or in a material control system (electronic or otherwise) are acceptable, but only under the conditions that it is impossible to inadvertently release or use a failed lot under the system. The supplier must demonstrate that the system provides adequate control.

The inspection and test status system should include positive controls that ensure that all required tests have been performed and appropriate action taken on the results.

Separate storage areas for quarantine of uninspected or nonconforming material, or special hold or day tanks for material awaiting testing are sometimes employed. When material is not held, as in the case of a process feeding directly into a pipeline or further process, on-line controls that ensure conformance of material may be used.

Figure 4.12-1 shows key decision steps.

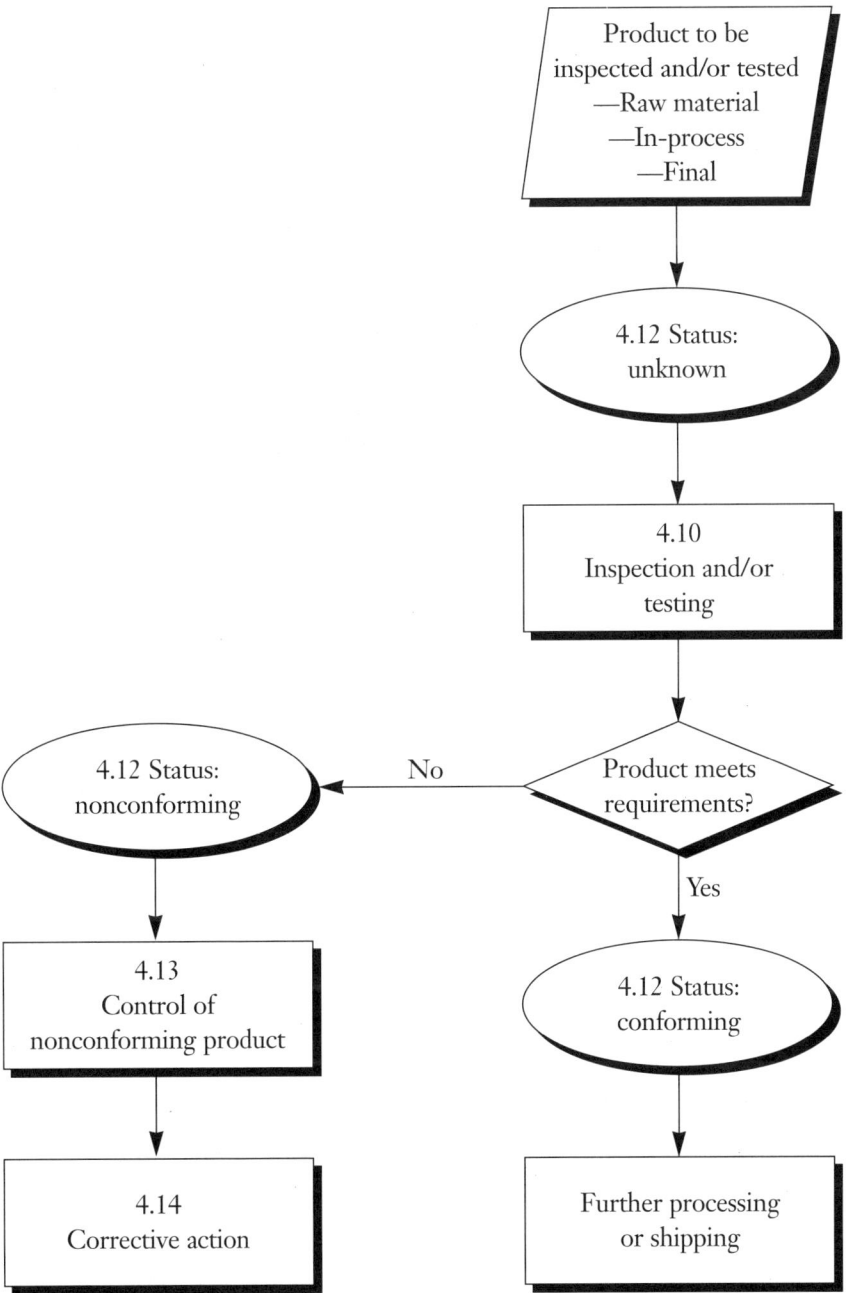

Figure 4.12-1. Inspection and test status.

4.13

Control of Nonconforming Product

Introduction

This clause of the standard requires procedures to prevent the unintended use or release of product for sale that does not conform to specifications or requirements. It also addresses review and distribution of nonconforming product.

> Q9001-1994 standard
>
> **4.13 CONTROL OF NONCONFORMING PRODUCT**
>
> **4.13.1 General**
>
> The supplier shall establish and maintain documented procedures to ensure that product that does not conform to specified requirements is prevented from unintended use or installation. This control shall provide for identification, documentation, evaluation, segregation (when practical), disposition of nonconforming product, and for notification to the functions concerned.

What's New?

- Procedures must be documented.

Guidance

Control systems need to be established that provide for identification, evaluation, segregation where practical, disposition, and documentation of nonconforming product, and for notification of other functions that may be affected including, where appropriate, the customer. The product control system must prevent the unintended use or shipment of nonconforming or uninspected product. Wherever practical, nonconforming or uninspected product should be physically segregated from conforming product or diverted and clearly identified.

In the CPI, product identification may be provided through

- Use of designated tanks or silos
- Notations in log or records
- Dedicated section of warehouse
- Marking or tagging
- Designated tank cars or trailers
- Product grading or classification systems

In the process industry, certain handling methods, such as pipeline distribution, may prevent segregation of nonconforming product. In such cases, trained and authorized personnel should use charts and records to control inventories and prevent inadvertent delivery or use. This may be accomplished electronically by computer control or through use of computer records. Regardless of method, the resulting system should be fail-safe.

Where products are moved by continuous flow, the absolute prevention of delivery of nonconforming product may not be practical. In this situation, the customer and the supplier should agree on an acceptable system for dealing with nonconformance. The supplier should establish emergency plans for immediately notifying the customer when the monitoring system indicates nonconformance and for interrupting the supply if the product is unacceptable to the customer. This may be appropriate in cases where the customer has the flexibility to tolerate slightly nonconforming product with sufficient notice to make compensating adjustments to the process. The supplier should also institute a rigorous system for control of the production process. It should include automatic and/or statistical process control (see clause 4.20) of key production process variables that affect product conformance to specifications or requirements. Where appropriate, this would also apply to variables that affect delivery (for example, pressure or temperature).

The supplier is required to document the event and notify appropriate personnel when nonconforming product is identified. This is conveniently done through the corrective action system. Depending on the supplier's defined criteria regarding the magnitude of the problem and the risks encountered, the corrective action process may be initiated (see clause 4.14).

Q9003 addresses only the identification, segregation, and documentation portions of this clause in 4.13.

Q9001-1994 standard

4.13.2 Review and disposition of nonconforming product

The responsibility for review and authority for the disposition of nonconforming product shall be defined.

Nonconforming product shall be reviewed in accordance with documented procedures. It may be

a) reworked to meet the specified requirements,

b) accepted with or without repair by concession,

c) regraded for alternative applications, or

d) rejected or scrapped.

Where required by the contract, the proposed use or repair of product (see 4.13.2b) which does not conform to specified requirements shall be reported for concession to the customer or customer's representative. The description of the nonconformity that has been accepted, and of repairs, shall be recorded to denote the actual condition (see 4.16).

Repaired and/or reworked product shall be reinspected in accordance with the quality plan and/or documented procedures.

What's New?

- Testing requirements for reworked product may be in the quality plan as well as in procedures.

Guidance

Personnel responsible for review and disposition of nonconforming product should be competent to evaluate the potential affects of disposition or action taken. This will include the effects of reworking, reprocessing, and so forth on performance, reliability, safety, aesthetics, and other measures.

Documented procedures should define the responsibility and authority of personnel to make disposition of nonconforming product. Review and disposition shall be in accordance with documented procedures. Records must be maintained of all nonconforming product and its disposition.

Disposition of nonconforming product may include

- Reworking to meet specifications or requirements. In the process industry, reworking may include reprocessing or adjusting of mixtures, including blending. These actions should follow established procedures to ensure that the resulting product fully complies with specified requirements. This should include testing for conformance to specifications in the same manner as the original material was tested (see Figure 4.12-1). Note, however, that in the CPI, rework is a frequent cause of product failures. For example, blending may bring one product property into specification while causing customer problems with other product characteristics.

- Accepting with or without reworking, by waiver of specification requirements by the customer. When offering nonconforming product for waiver, the supplier should provide a written document describing the nature of the nonconformance(s) and any rework performed. Evidence of customer agreement should be available. If such agreement is verbal, the supplier should document the discussion, including who approved what nonconformities, when, and so on.

- Regrading for alternative applications where product does meet requirements (for example, regrading from food to industrial grade).

- Rejecting or scrapping, which carries the least risk from the customer's point of view, but often the highest cost.

Records of all nonconformities and their disposition should be maintained with appropriate identification of the lots, items, time periods, production facility, results of all testing or inspections, and so forth, along with identification of individuals authorizing disposition. These records should contain all information essential to allow auditing of the system and for taking corrective action to prevent recurrence of the nonconformity.

Q9003 addresses only the reinspection requirements of this clause.

4.14

Corrective and Preventive Action

Introduction

This clause of the standard addresses having a documented corrective and preventive action system for nonconformances in products, processes, or systems. In addition, the necessity for taking preventive action is included as part of an overall continuous improvement system. The underlying purpose of this clause is to eliminate the causes of nonconforming products and services by taking preventive or corrective actions to prevent occurrence or recurrence of problems in the quality system.

There is often some confusion about the difference between corrective and preventive action. The two terms are defined in ANSI/ISO/ASQC A8402-1994 (emphasis added).

> *Corrective action* is action taken to eliminate the cause of an *existing* nonconformity, defect or other undesirable situation in order to *prevent recurrence*.
>
> NOTES:
>
> 1. The corrective actions may involve changes, such as in procedures and systems, to achieve quality improvement at any stage of the quality loop.

2. There is a distinction between "correction" and "corrective action": *Correction* refers to repair, rework or adjustment and relates to the disposition of an existing nonconformity. *Corrective action* relates to the elimination of the causes of a nonconformity.

Preventive action is action taken to eliminate the causes of a *potential* nonconformity, defect or other undesirable situation in order to *prevent occurrence*.

NOTE:

1. The preventive actions may involve changes, such as in procedures and systems, to achieve quality improvement at any stage of the quality loop.

It is important to understand that the distinction is not short- versus long-term action. Corrective action is *reactive*, while preventive action is *proactive*. Both corrective and preventive action are preventive in nature: corrective action prevents recurrence, while preventive action prevents occurrence.

When considering product nonconformity, a further distinction can be made between clauses 4.13 and 4.14. Clause 4.13 addresses the (short-term) handling and disposition of the product itself, while 4.14 does not. Clause 4.14 is primarily concerned with the underlying cause of the nonconformity and the elimination of its cause so as to prevent a recurrence of the event. The standard emphasizes finding root causes. This is above and beyond the immediate actions (corrections) that may be taken to treat the symptoms.

Q9001-1994 standard

4.14 CORRECTIVE AND PREVENTIVE ACTION

4.14.1 General

The supplier shall establish and maintain documented procedures for implementing corrective and preventive action.

> Any corrective or preventive action taken to eliminate the causes of actual or potential nonconformities shall be to a degree appropriate to the magnitude of problems and commensurate with the risks encountered.
>
> The supplier shall implement and record any changes to the documented procedures resulting from corrective and preventive action.

What's New?
- **Procedures are now required to address both corrective and preventive actions.**

Guidance

The revised 1994 standard has two distinct sections: (1) corrective action and (2) preventive action. The objective of both is to have a documented prevention-based process that encompasses the entire quality system from receipt of material from a subcontractor through delivery of product or services. Documented procedures should define how nonconformities are identified, documented, and resolved.

There is somewhat of a loophole in the phrase "appropriate to the magnitude of problems and commensurate with the risks encountered." The standard recognizes that the supplier's judgment must be applied in deciding which problems warrant a thorough root cause analysis and actions to eliminate the cause. For example: management may elect not to take action on a single process-related problem of low cost and risk to the company or customer due to more frequent or more costly issues that the company faces.

Problems should be prioritized. Resourcing should be considered in defining criteria for which types of nonconformances will receive the full treatment of corrective action.

It is expected that the company will be able to demonstrate that changes made are documented, implemented, and that the effectiveness of the action is verified.

> **Q9001-1994 standard**
>
> **4.14.2 Corrective action**
>
> The procedures for corrective action shall include:
>
> a) the effective handling of customer complaints and reports of product nonconformities;
>
> b) investigation of the cause of nonconformities relating to product, process, and quality system, and recording the results of the investigation (see 4.16);
>
> c) determination of the corrective action needed to eliminate the cause of nonconformities;
>
> d) application of controls to ensure that corrective action is taken and that it is effective.

What's New?

- Requirements for corrective action system have been more clearly defined.
- **The scope has been expanded to include not only product nonconformities, but also customer complaints and problems with processes and the quality system itself.**

Guidance

Complaints from customers must be effectively handled according to procedures. Some organizations have attempted to avoid documenting complaints by calling them "concerns" or "issues," unless the customer explicitly uses the word *complaint*. In the spirit of driving true quality improvement, the supplier should define complaint broadly, for example, as anything that was not what the customer wanted.

Other quality-related problems that must be handled include nonconforming product, complaints to vendors or subcontractors, and deficiencies detected during quality audits.

Within the manufacturing operations, the supplier should clearly define criteria for what types of events require documentation of the event and corrective actions taken. For example, process upsets may occur due to sporadic events such as weather or equipment failures that the supplier does not desire to formally document in the corrective action system. Chronic recurring problems, however, or those with a large impact, should be documented to promote continuous improvement. Responsibilities for corrective and preventive actions should be defined within procedures for various parts of the quality system.

Every organization needs to have effective systems for handling customer complaints and reporting product nonconformities. These procedures should delineate the responsibility and authority for recording, reporting, coordinating, assigning, and implementing corrective action and for responding to customers. Many times the responsibility for the recording, reporting, assignment, and coordination of such activities lies within the quality function, while the responsibility for identifying the cause and implementing corrective action lies with the departments where the problem occurred.

Often analysis of the problem and implementation of the actions will involve a team composed of the functions involved in the process. Subclause 4.14.2b calls for an investigation phase of the corrective action process to ensure that the underlying cause is identified prior to taking action. The results of the investigation should be recorded along with the appropriate corrective actions taken. Quite often the actions taken will be reflected in changes to operating procedures or work instructions to prevent recurrence.

An example of corrective action for nonconforming product is

Statement type	Statement
Nonconformity	Batch 95342 was high in acid content.
Correction	The batch was treated with caustic to bring the pH within specifications. (Note that the correction will not prevent recurrence of the incident).
Root cause	A series of statistically designed experiments indicated that the acid quantity as stated in batch instructions was 4 percent too high.
Corrective action	Reduced acid level by 4 percent in rev. 3 of batch instructions, dated 6/16/95.

An example of corrective action for a customer complaint is

Statement type	Statement
Nonconformity	XYZ Co. complained that product A was delivered instead of product B.
Correction	Authorized return of product A and delivered product B the next day.
Root cause	Discovered software error in order entry system.
Corrective action	Changed product database information for XYZ Co.

In addition, nonconformities related to the quality system, such as internal audit nonconformities (see clause 4.17), must be addressed as part of the corrective action system. The standard requires follow-up to ensure that the action was actually taken and was effective. The internal audit system is often used as this control method. Note that these follow-up activities will occur after the passage of sufficient time to collect objective evidence that the cause has in fact been eliminated and the problem has not recurred. That is, it will typically occur months, not days later. Records of the corrective action and verification should be maintained.

Q9001-1994 standard

4.14.3 Preventive action

The procedures for preventive action shall include:

a) the use of appropriate sources of information such as processes and work operations which affect product quality, concessions, audit results, quality records, service reports, and customer complaints to detect, analyze, and eliminate potential causes of nonconformities;

b) determination of the steps needed to deal with any problems requiring preventive action;

> c) initiation of preventive action and application of controls to ensure that it is effective;
>
> d) ensuring that relevant information on actions taken is submitted for management review (see 4.1.3).

What's New?

- **This is a new subclause. Preventive actions were not explicitly required in the 1987 standard.**
- **Information must be submitted for management review.**

Guidance

Preventive action as defined by the standard addresses going the extra step to improve the quality system before problems occur. Specifically, a lot of data are generated from key quality and business activities and should be analyzed to detect potential problems or trends. One should consider the need for statistical techniques in this analysis (see clause 4.20.1). The types of data that can provide useful information about the quality system are

- Quality test and inspection data
- Process information from control charts of key process variables
- Internal audit results
- Management reviews
- Subcontractor performance data
- Customer satisfaction surveys
- Equipment maintenance information
- Calibration records and instrument control charts
- Cost of quality
- Employee suggestions
- Employee surveys
- Statistical capability measures

- Contingency plans
- Risk analysis

Periodic analyses of these sources of data can be most useful in eliminating trends or causes of potential nonconformances. As in corrective action, the appropriate steps to be taken to prevent problems are dependent on the nature and severity of the problem to the business and resources available to address the problem. Pareto analysis, cause-and-effect analysis, and other problem-solving methodologies can be used by teams in identifying and analyzing potential problems.

These problems are often cross-functional in nature and require team solutions and implementation to provide effective improvement of the system. Permanent changes resulting from the actions should be recorded in operating procedures, work instructions, manufacturing processes, product specifications, and the quality system. Ensuring that the solution has been implemented and is effective provides verification per subclause 4.14.3c. Records of the results of the investigation and verification of the effectiveness of the solution are required, as with corrective action. Recognize, however, that verifying the effectiveness of preventive action is a bit more difficult than it is with corrective action.

Subclause 4.14.3d addresses the need for relevant preventive action information to be reported to the management review process. Technically, the standard only refers to preventive action, but it is recommended that corrections, corrective actions, and preventive actions be addressed in management review so that senior managers are aware as to how the quality system is functioning and so that priorities can be established and appropriate resources provided. Follow-up on actions taken should be part of the review on major action items to ensure that the actions are being carried out and that they are effective.

Q9003 requires only corrective, not preventive action, and does not require procedures. It applies only to final inspection and to customer complaints regarding the product itself.

4.15

Handling, Storage, Packaging, Preservation, and Delivery

Introduction

This clause of the standard addresses the distribution of incoming, in-process, and finished products. In the CPI, it is often beneficial to apply these criteria to raw materials and intermediates if not addressed in clause 4.9, Process Control. From a pragmatic view, packaging, preservation, and delivery apply mostly to finished product. Also, pragmatically, storage and handling requirements apply throughout the process.

> Q9001-1994 standard
>
> **4.15 HANDLING, STORAGE, PACKAGING, PRESERVATION, AND DELIVERY**
>
> **4.15.1 General**
>
> The supplier shall establish and maintain documented procedures for handling, storage, packaging, preservation, and delivery of product.

What's New?

- This subclause has been slightly revised for clarity.

Guidance

The requirements of this clause of the standard are equally applicable to the supplier and supplier-controlled subcontractors (terminal operator, transporter, distributors, and so on). The customer may even have a role depending on where ownership transfer occurs (for example, supplier loads carrier, then customer owns product). The distinction between the quality systems needed by each lies in the product-handling functions they perform and the responsibilities they have as defined by contractual agreements relative to product distribution processes.

Q9001-1994 standard

4.15.2 Handling

The supplier shall provide methods of handling product that prevent damage or deterioration.

What's New?

- This subclause has been slightly revised for clarity.

Guidance

Handling in the chemical and process industries involves many transfers of bulk or packaged product from raw material receipt through production and acceptance of finished product by the customer. All means of handling, including the use of pallets, containers, conveyors, vessels, tanks, pipelines, and vehicles are to be addressed in the supplier's system. The supplier should ensure that product is handled so that product quality is maintained. Documented procedures should govern product as it is being distributed to ensure that

- Products are not inadvertently mixed.
- Contamination does not occur.
- Product is protected from change other than normal aging.

Handling procedures should ensure that the potential for contamination, reaction, and/or degradation is minimized or eliminated. Packages or other containers should be inspected before product filling or loading to ensure the integrity of the container and the absence of manufacturing residues, contaminants, or other foreign material. Sampling of reusable containers may be required to determine if the "heel" might contaminate incoming product (see clause 4.10.2).

Pipeline and loading systems should, if possible, be dedicated to specific products and positively isolated from all sources of contamination. If not dedicated, detailed changeover or line clearing procedures may be required to ensure that product quality is maintained (for example, header systems or shared loading and transfer systems). Sequencing of products shipped is sometimes used to minimize the effects of residuals. Plug flow conditions may allow for accurate splitting between products based on density.

Methods for product identification (records and/or labeling, where appropriate) should provide durable information for traceability throughout all handling processes and on to delivery at the customer (see clause 4.8).

When practical, a lot should be segregated before testing and not commingled with other production. During transfer of contents of a rundown, bulk storage, or shipping tank to smaller containers, the larger vessel should be thoroughly mixed and totally isolated from any streams or inputs that might change the quality of that lot.

All interruptions to filling or loading of a bulk product should be documented in production records for later use in process control and problem resolution. If the filling or loading operation of a bulk product is significantly interrupted on either a planned or unplanned basis, then samples may need to be taken and tested to determine if the product still conforms to specifications. The need to resample and retest should be based on the characteristics of the specific product and the specific loading and filling process.

Q9001-1994 standard

4.15.3 Storage

The supplier shall use designated storage areas or stock rooms to prevent damage or deterioration of product, pending use or delivery.

> Appropriate methods for authorizing receipt to and dispatch from such areas shall be stipulated.
>
> In order to detect deterioration, the condition of product in stock shall be assessed at appropriate intervals.

What's New?

- This subclause has been slightly revised for clarity.

Guidance

The supplier needs to ensure that product is stored under conditions that do not cause deterioration or change the quality of the product beyond normal aging. Maintenance procedures for storage vessels should address the potential for environmental contamination (see clause 4.9g).

Storage containers in the CPI may include tanks, caverns, tank cars, hopper cars, box cars, bags, boxes, warehouses, silos, and piles. Storage containers should be selected with consideration given to

- Materials of construction
- Pressure rating
- Storage temperature
- Storage capacity
- Corrosion
- Contamination potential
- Previous contents
- Loading facilities
- Product characteristics

Procedures should be documented for receipt, transfer, and changing production or service of storage containers from one product to another. Products in storage need to be checked periodically to detect possible deterioration. Rotation of stock and shelf life need to be considered in CPI storage procedures.

> Q9001-1994 standard
>
> **4.15.4 Packaging**
>
> The supplier shall control packing, packaging, and marking processes (including materials used) to the extent necessary to ensure conformance to specified requirements.

What's New?

- This part of this subclause has not been changed.

Guidance

CPI products that are not distributed in bulk are often shipped in discrete packages such as drums, boxes, bales, or crates. Recyclable packaging materials are often used.

The specific package design should be carefully selected. Considerations include potential for corrosion and deterioration as well as previous contents, loading and unloading facilities, and product characteristics. Preventive action might consist of evaluation of options to anticipate potential conditions where damage or loss might occur.

Procedures should be defined and documented to ensure that quality is maintained during packaging. Package cleanliness, to prevent possible contamination, and package integrity, to prevent possible loss and injury, must be addressed. Inspection plans and responsibilities of the product manufacturer, packaging subcontractor, and transporter should be documented and communicated.

Dedicated containers may reduce some quality concerns while raising others such as careful planning and implementation to avoid container shortages economically.

Packages should be labeled, according to the specifications and applicable regulations (see clause 4.8). Marking and labeling should be legible and durable.

Containers that cannot be physically labeled with product identification, such as rail cars, trucks, barges, pipelines, and other bulk containers, should be uniquely identified on records such as bills of lading and the certificate of analysis. They should be placarded as appropriate to meet safety requirements.

> Q9001-1994 standard
>
> **4.15.5 Preservation**
>
> The supplier shall apply appropriate methods for preservation and segregation of product when the product is under the supplier's control.

What's New?

- **The existing requirement was separated out as new subclause.**

Guidance

Methods for preservation of the quality attributes of product must be provided. In the CPI, examples include dedicated tankage and piping, blanketing of storage vessels, control of pH, and addition of preservatives. Products with unusual storage and handling requirements, such as specific temperature ranges, must be accommodated. Product segregation is a common practice. Special preservation requirements should be identified on packaging, or other appropriate documentation.

Products with limited shelf life or requiring special protection during transport or storage should be identified and procedures maintained to ensure deteriorated products are not put into use. In some cases, the packaging materials, rather than the product, may be the limiting factor for shelf life.

> Q9001-1994 standard
>
> **4.15.6 Delivery**
>
> The supplier shall arrange for the protection of the quality of product after final inspection and test. Where contractually specified, this protection shall be extended to include delivery to destination.

What's New?

- There are no changes to this subclause.

Guidance

Transporters include railroads, trucking agencies, pipeline operators, shipping agencies, terminal operators, and freight forwarders. The contract should specify the extent to which the supplier, the transportation subcontractor, and the customer are each obligated to protect product quality during delivery.

When common carriers are used, the customer is customarily responsible for protecting product quality when the customer has arranged the shipment. Although the customer may be paying for the common carrier, the supplier customarily has responsibility for protecting product quality when the supplier arranges the shipment. Supplier may also have a role in protecting the integrity of the shipment through control of weight distribution, provision of dunnage, and so on.

Provision for protecting product quality is important during all phases of delivery. Consider the various methods of delivery and variations in environmental conditions that may be encountered during delivery. The customer should ensure that unloading procedures, equipment, lines, and storage will not jeopardize product integrity. A quality requirement (clause 4.3) might be that the packaging must prevent spills.

For time-sensitive products, including services, delivery time is a critical factor. When this is the case, procedures must ensure acceptable delivery time.

In-transit product transfers during product shipments should be avoided. Contamination, damage, and loss are risks of in-transit product transfers. If an emergency situation leads to a transfer, the responsible carrier or terminal must receive clear and complete transfer instructions from the supplier. (Note: In-transit transfers of less-than-truckload [LTL] shipments of packaged goods are common and acceptable practice.)

If product (or the container) is damaged or exposed to potential contamination, the supplier should be contacted immediately. Under no circumstances should spilled or damaged product be repackaged and delivered to the customer without proper authority.

Pipeline transfers of product directly to customers present unique quality control situations. Quality of product should be monitored with methods and frequencies agreed upon by the customer and the supplier. All inputs to pipelines should be well identified. The quality of each input should be monitored on a basis agreed upon with the customers.

If multiple suppliers use common pipelines, effective common procedures for quality assurance must be documented and used by all product suppliers, pipeline subcontractors, and customers. Compliance to these procedures should be audited.

4.16

Control of Quality Records

Introduction

This clause of the standard discusses the required record-keeping system. Refer to clause 4.5 guidance for a description of the difference between records and documents.

> Q9001-1994 standard
>
> **4.16 CONTROL OF QUALITY RECORDS**
>
> The supplier shall establish and maintain documented procedures for identification, collection, indexing, access, filing, storage, maintenance, and disposition of quality records.
>
> Quality records shall be maintained to demonstrate conformance to specified requirements and the effective operation of the quality system. Pertinent quality records from the subcontractor shall be an element of these data.
>
> All quality records shall be legible and shall be stored and retained in such a way that they are readily retrievable in facilities that provide a suitable environment to prevent damage or deterioration and to prevent loss. Retention times of quality records shall be established and recorded. Where agreed contractually, quality records shall be made

> available for evaluation by the customer or the customer's representative for an agreed period.
>
> NOTE 19 Records may be in the form of any type of media, such as hard copy or electronic media.

What's New?

- Procedures must now be documented.
- Note 19 has been added.

Guidance

The supplier should maintain adequate records to demonstrate achievement of the required quality and to verify effective operation of the supplier's quality system. The supplier may choose more than one medium (for example, paper, electronic, or microfilm) for record storage. The methods must provide for timely retrieval of records and security as appropriate. Whatever medium is selected, the records should be protected from loss, damage, and deterioration due to environmental conditions.

The supplier must define the types of quality records that need to be kept. The following types of records are specifically referred to in this standard.

ANSI/ISO/ ASQC Q9001 clause	Records to be maintained*
4.1.3	Management review
4.2.3h	Quality planning
4.3.4	Contract review
4.4.6	Design review
4.4.7	Design verification
4.6.2c	Acceptable subcontractors
4.7	Customer-supplied product that becomes lost, damaged, or otherwise unsuitable for use

ANSI/ISO/ ASQC Q9001 clause	Records to be maintained*
4.8	Unique product identification
4.9	Qualified processes, equipment, and personnel
4.10.2.3	Identification of material released under positive recall procedure
4.10.5	Inspection and test records, including release authority
4.11.1	Checks of test software or comparative references
4.11.2e	Calibrations of inspection, measuring, and test equipment
4.13.2	Nonconforming product
4.14.2b	Results of investigation of nonconformities
4.17	Audit results
4.17	Follow-up audit verification activities
4.18	Training records

*This list includes those clauses that reference clause 4.16. There are other parts of the standard such as clause 4.6.2b that require records, but do not include a reference to 4.16.

The supplier should decide and document retention times for quality records appropriate to the type of record. Consider these factors in setting retention times.

- Requirements of the contract with the customer
- Applicable legal or regulatory requirements (for example, FDA)
- The stated useful life of the purchased product
- Corporate record retention policies and guidelines

Process data are increasingly recorded by on-line computer systems in the chemical industry. If these records are maintained to demonstrate the effectiveness of the quality system, the supplier should

- Verify that software meets the quality system needs
- Verify the accuracy and precision of recorded values

- Screen the records for missing or abnormal observations
- Protect old records from being written over by new records
- Create archives of electronic records to assure recovery when required

The supplier must also document the procedures followed for collection, indexing, access, storage, maintenance, and disposition of quality records. For instance, the disposition of records that have exceeded their retention times may need to be defined. These records may be moved to off-site storage, microfilmed, or destroyed.

Q9003 addresses only records required to substantiate conformance with specified requirements for finished product.

4.17

Internal Quality Audits

Introduction

While internal auditing is a familiar concept in the world of finance, it may not be for quality. ANSI/ISO/ASQC A8402-1994 and Q10011 provide a key definition.

> **quality audit:** systematic and independent examination to determine whether quality activities and related results comply with planned arrangements and whether these arrangements are implemented effectively and are suitable to achieve objectives.

The term *planned arrangements* refers to any and all requirements, including: customer contracts, quality system standards (for example, Q9001), government regulations, specifications, as well as the supplier's own policies, procedures, and plans. Note especially the inclusion of "related results" and verification that the systems have been "implemented effectively."

Over and above this formal definition, internal quality audits should be thought of as a management tool. It is a means for collecting factual, objective information about one's quality system and its effectiveness. This information is a vital element in driving quality improvement, which is (or should be) the fundamental purpose of the quality system.

Internal quality audits should focus on evaluating the adequacy of the quality system as a whole, as well as each of the elements in the system. This can be contrasted with quality control activities, which employ various quality technology tools and procedures to achieve the desired results in specific parts of the quality system. Quality system audits also differ from management reviews (see clause 4.1.3), which review audit reports along with other sources of information to determine how well the quality system is functioning and to initiate any needed changes. While this clause of the standard does not exclude auditing of products and production process technical aspects, audits of the supplier's quality system itself are the minimum requirement and the focus for compliance with Q9001.

Q9001-1994 standard

4.17 INTERNAL QUALITY AUDITS

The supplier shall establish and maintain documented procedures for planning and implementing internal quality audits to verify whether quality activities and related results comply with planned arrangements and to determine the effectiveness of the quality system.

Internal quality audits shall be scheduled on the basis of the status and importance of the activity to be audited and shall be carried out by personnel independent of those having direct responsibility for the activity being audited.

The results of the audits shall be recorded (see 4.16) and brought to the attention of the personnel having responsibility in the area audited. The management personnel responsible for the area shall take timely corrective action on deficiencies found during the audit.

Follow-up audit activities shall verify and record the implementation and effectiveness of the corrective action taken (see 4.16).

NOTES

20 The results of internal quality audits form an integral part of the input to management review activities (see 4.1.3).

21 Guidance on quality-system audits is given in ANSI/ISO/ASQC Q10011-1-1994, ANSI/ISO/ASQC Q10011-2-1994, and ANSI/ISO/ASQC Q10011-3-1994.

What's New?

- This clause clarifies that procedures must now be documented.
- **Follow-up activities to verify implementation and effectiveness are now explicitly required versus implied.**
- Notes 20 and 21 have been added.

Guidance

An internal quality system audit function begins with a management policy describing its scope, responsibility, and authority, and requiring auditees (audited areas) to cooperate during audits and to carry out corrective actions. There should be written procedures for planning, carrying out, reporting, documenting, and following up audits, and also for selecting, training, and qualifying auditors. Prioritize activities by considering

- How critical they are to the quality of the product
- The results of previous audits
- How difficult the activities are to keep in control

There should be a schedule of periodic audits that reflects these priorities. Areas having problems should be audited more frequently and all parts of the system should be audited at least annually.

Auditors must be trained personnel (see clause 4.1.2.2 and clause 4.18). While the supplier is completely free to define the appropriate training requirements, the following suggestions may be helpful.

Course	Typical length	Priority	Who should attend?
Lead auditor training	4½ days	1	Audit program manager
		2	Internal lead auditors
		3	Persons conducting second-party audits of subcontractors
		4	Auditors desiring external certification
Internal quality auditing	2–3 days	1	All internal quality auditors

It is recommended that at least one person (in, say, a 100-person organization) attend the lead auditor training. This person may then make a recommendation whether additional individuals should also attend. Training should include knowledge of the content of the Q9000 series and the auditing techniques Q10011. It is also recommended that lead auditor training courses be accredited by the U.S. Registrar Accreditation Board or other internationally recognized equivalent.

External auditor certification is not necessary (or even recommended) for internal auditors. It may, however, be a useful credential when auditing subcontractors, and it is the norm among third-party auditors.

Both lead auditors and audit team members should be as independent as is practical from the area being audited. They should also have the necessary qualifications and experience to fulfill their roles on the team. It is useful to have operators or others familiar with work operations to serve on the audit team.

The team collects objective evidence during the audit, focusing on procedures, work instructions and records, the facility and equipment, and observation of work being performed. The evidence should show both what is working as intended and what needs to be corrected. An audit should conclude with a meeting with the auditee's management, at which time the lead auditor presents audit observations and overall conclusions regarding the quality system. The focus should encompass not only compliance, but also improvement, since internal auditors have more license to suggest efficiency and productivity improvement opportunities than do third party auditors.

The results of the audit must be documented. The team should report the audit results to management having the authority and responsibility to take corrective action and to the auditee's management. Records should indicate that the audit results were considered during management review.

The auditee is responsible for determining and carrying out actions to correct the deficiencies. Usually the goal is to identify actions that will eliminate the root cause of deficiencies and thus prevent their recurrence (see also clause 4.14.2). The time necessary to complete the actions is normally agreed to by responsible management and the auditee in consultation with the auditors.

Follow-up activities are required. The purpose is to verify that corrective actions have indeed been implemented and that such actions have proven effective in preventing the recurrence of the deficiency. The audit function typically maintains a responsibility to follow up after an appropriate period of time. The results of the follow-up must be recorded and should indicate

- Implementation of corrective action
- Determination of the effectiveness of the implemented corrective action

Q9003 requires internal audits for systems covered by that standard.

4.18

Training

Introduction

This clause describes the requirements for ensuring that personnel are trained and skilled to perform their tasks and activities that affect quality.

Q9001-1994 standard

4.18 TRAINING

The supplier shall establish and maintain documented procedures for identifying training needs and provide for the training of all personnel performing activities affecting quality. Personnel performing specific assigned tasks shall be qualified on the basis of appropriate education, training, and/or experience, as required. Appropriate records of training shall be maintained (see 4.16).

What's New?

- Procedures must now be documented.

Guidance

The documented procedures addressing training of personnel should indicate how the training needs of employees are identified and how subsequent training is provided. In the chemical and process industries, this is frequently accomplished through job descriptions, checklists, and/or training on standard operating procedures and work instructions. Management review (clause 4.1.3), corrective action (clause 4.14), and internal quality audits (clause 4.17) are areas that may identify needs for additional training. It may also be advisable to conduct training surveys and/or performance reviews on a periodic basis, in which employees may indicate the training they believe they need.

Other training requirements that may apply to CPI include training on statistical techniques, ANSI/ISO/ASQC Q9000 series standards, internal auditing, process safety management, and process control systems. Additionally, some personnel in the plant may require certification, such as welders and boiler operators. Be aware that if training is provided in-house, instructors need to be able to demonstrate their qualifications to provide the training.

This clause of the ANSI/ISO/ASQC Q9001 standard requires that individuals be qualified for their functions based on education, training, and/or experience. Evidence of this qualification could be through the evaluation of a trainer or a supervisor, or through completion of a written, verbal, or performance exam. In some instances, qualifications may be met through professional degrees or prior work experience. A method for evaluating employee performance should be developed.

Records of training must be maintained in accordance with the requirements of clause 4.16. These records should clearly show that employees have completed all required training and achieved subsequent qualification.

4.19

Servicing

Introduction

This clause of the standard covers all aspects of service, either before or after the sale, that are defined in the customer's contract.

> Q9001-1994 standard
>
> **4.19 SERVICING**
>
> Where servicing is a specified requirement, the supplier shall establish and maintain documented procedures for performing, verifying, and reporting that the servicing meets the specified requirements.

What's New?

- Procedures must be documented and must include reporting, performing, and verifying service work.
- **This clause is now included as a requirement in Q9002.**

Guidance

The standard does not refer to the normal service/technical assistance activities by the supplier that are common business practices, nor to the provision of a service, unless specified in a contract. Services covered by this clause are typically paid for by the customer on a separate basis from the product that is being serviced. Contractual requirements for servicing define the supplier's responsibility to help the customer ensure proper use of the product following delivery. Should the supplier choose to include noncontractual technical services, procedures for this might be developed along the line of requirements of the clause.

In the hard goods or mechanical industries, servicing means repair, maintenance, upgrading, and so on. In the chemical and process industries, servicing occurs where there is an ongoing relationship between the supplier and customer relating to the performance of the product after its delivery. Examples might include water treatment, catalyst supply, and licensing of technology.

Required servicing should be documented in a plan agreed to by the supplier and customer. This document should clearly outline the responsibilities of the supplier, the customer, and any third parties. The procedures may refer to

- Specialized handling and test equipment needed, and its maintenance and control
- How the customer's complaints and/or special requests are to be resolved
- A performance specification for the product or service
- The particular operating, control, inspection, and testing procedures used to verify the performance of the service
- Back-up provisions including technical assistance and the availability of alternate equipment or materials
- Training and qualification of appropriate supplier personnel
- The planning of service activities
- How to contact supplier's personnel in case of emergency
- How the service report is to be documented and distributed

In effect, all relevant clauses of the standard should be applied to servicing, just as if it were the only product being provided to the customer.

Q9003 does not cover servicing.

4.20

Statistical Techniques

Introduction

This clause of the standard addresses the use of statistical tools for controlling processes and determining process capability to ensure the ability to meet customer's contractual requirements.

> Q9001-1994 standard
>
> **4.20 STATISTICAL TECHNIQUES**
>
> **4.20.1 Identification of need**
>
> The supplier shall identify the need for statistical techniques required for establishing, controlling, and verifying process capability and product characteristics.

What's New?
- The clause has been broadened and divided into two sections, one to identify the need for statistical techniques and a second to document how those techniques are to be used.

Guidance

This clause of the standard asks the supplier to identify the need for statistical techniques that are important in controlling processes so that the customers' requirements can be met. In most process industries, statistical techniques are widely applicable to monitor and control critical process and product quality characteristics. It is important that a good deal of thought be given as to what these parameters are and how best to apply the appropriate statistical techniques to assure the quality of the products offered.

Statistical methods are often used to characterize the process, product, and measurement system variability using analytical test results and inspection data. This implies that the supplier has to know the capabilities of the processes in order to be able to discern ability to meet those requirements prior to accepting the contract or order. C_p or C_{pk} are commonly used as a measure of process capability in the process industries, while P_p and P_{pk} are used as measures of process performance. These are quite useful when applied properly.

Clause 4.4.5, Design Output, requires that companies "identify those characteristics crucial to the safe and proper functioning of the product." This identification of key process control parameters and product characteristics in the design phase of a project implies that these are prime candidates for the application of statistical control techniques to ensure the product is produced in a controlled, consistent manner. Typical statistical techniques include

- Use of simple statistics, such as average and standard deviation as point estimates
- Shewhart charts
- Process capability and performance indices
- Trend charts
- Pareto diagrams
- Scatter plots
- Histograms
- Analysis of variance
- Design of experiments

Statistical techniques may be used to
- Establish sampling plans
- Make decisions on conformance to requirements
- Study process capability
- Determine measurement capability
- Determine when test equipment may require maintenance or calibration
- Monitor key process/product characteristics
- Compare subcontractor capabilities
- Analyze data for improvement opportunities
- Evaluate customer complaint trends
- Analyze causes of nonconformances
- Prepare performance reports to management and customers
- Analyze timeliness of shipments or deliveries

Q9001-1994 standard

4.20.2 Procedures

The supplier shall establish and maintain documented procedures to implement and control the application of the statistical techniques identified in 4.20.1.

What's New?
- **The subclause now clarifies that needed procedures must be documented and implemented.**

Guidance

When the need for statistical techniques has been identified, procedures must be documented on how they are to be implemented and then used. The introduction of statistical techniques into an organization should include a thorough grounding and training for those people expected to use them effectively (see clause 4.18). These people would be expected to be able to explain the proper use of such techniques and how they are being used to improve the quality system.

Documented procedures should describe how the statistical techniques identified are used to control and improve the product or verify that the process is capable. This would include actions to be taken by the people using these techniques to bring the product or process into control.

Often, companies use statistical techniques to analyze management information such as complaints, rework, rejected product, and so on. The analysis and review of this data becomes part of the management review process and is used for problem identification and problem solving.

Appendix A

Sources for Ordering Standards

ASQC
611 East Wisconsin Avenue
P.O. Box 3005
Milwaukee, WI 53201-3005
Telephone: 414-272-8575 or 800-248-1946
Fax: 414-272-1734

American National Standards Institute (ANSI)
Attention: Customer Service
11 West 42nd Street
New York, NY 10036
Telephone: 212-642-4900
Fax: 212-302-1286

Appendix B

Acronyms

ANSI .... American National Standards Institute
API .... American Petroleum Institute
ASME .... American Society of Mechanical Engineering
ASQC .... American Society for Quality Control
ASTM .... American Society for Testing and Materials
CIC .... Chemical Interest Committee of CPID
CPI .... Chemical and Process Industries
CPID .... Chemical and Process Industry Division of ASQC
DoD .... U.S. Department of Defense
EN .... European norm
EU .... European Union
FDA .... U.S. Food and Drug Administration
GMP .... Good Manufacturing Practices
IEC .... International Electrotechnical Commission
ISO .... International Organization for Standardization
MIL STD ... Military standard
RAB .... Registrar Accreditation Board
OSHA .... Occupational Safety and Health Administration
USDA .... U.S. Department of Agriculture
TC .... Technical committee

Reprinted with permission from ISO 9000 Registered Company Directory, published by Irwin Professional in Fairfax, VA.

Appendix C

Quality Management and Quality Assurance Standards

Standard	Title	Brief description of contents
ANSI/ISO/ ASQC A8402-1994	*Quality Management and Quality Assurance—Vocabulary*	Clarifies and standardizes the quality terms as they apply to the field of quality management. Defines the fundamental terms relating to quality concepts as they apply to all areas for the preparation and use of quality-related standards and for mutual understanding in international communications.
ANSI/ISO/ ASQC Q9000-1-1994	*Quality Management and Quality Assurance Standards—Guidelines for Selection and Use*	Provides guidance for the selection and use of this family of international standards on quality management and quality assurance. Clarifies the principal quality-related concepts needed for effective understanding and application of the standards, and the distinctions and interrelationships between them.
ANSI/ISO/ ASQC Q9000-2-1993	*Quality Management and Quality Assurance Standards—Generic Guidelines for the Application of ANSI/ISO/ASQC Q9001, Q9002, and Q9003*	Provides guidelines to enable users to have improved consistency, precision, clarity, and understanding when applying the requirements of the ISO 9000 series of standards.

Standard	Title	Brief description of contents
ANSI/ISO/ ASQC Q9000-3-1991	*Guidelines for the Application of ANSI/ ISO/ASQC Q9001 to the Development, Supply, and Maintenance of Software*	Provides guidelines to software developers, suppliers, maintainers, and purchasers in the specification and implementation of ISO 9001 quality system requirements as applied to software.
ISO 9000-4-1993	*Quality Management and Quality Assurance Standards—Part 4: Guide to Dependability Program Management*	Provides guidelines for the planning, organization, direction, and control of resources to produce products that will be reliable and maintainable. This part of IEC 300/ISO 9000 is applicable to hardware and/or software products, primarily at controlling influences on dependability at all product life-cycle phases from product planning to operation.
ANSI/ISO/ ASQC Q9001-1994	*Quality Systems—Model for Quality Assurance in Design, Development, Production, Installation, and Servicing*	This standard specifies quality system requirements for use where a supplier's capability to design and supply conforming product needs to be demonstrated. The requirements specified are aimed primarily at achieving customer satisfaction by preventing nonconformity at all stages from design through to servicing. This standard is applicable in situations when —Design is required and the product requirements are stated principally in performance terms, or they need to be established —Confidence in product conformance can be attained by adequate demonstration of a supplier's capabilities in design, development, production, installation, and servicing

Standard	Title	Brief description of contents
ANSI/ISO/ ASQC Q9002-1994	*Quality Systems— Model for Quality Assurance in Design, Development, Production, Installation, and Servicing*	This standard specifies quality system requirements for use where a supplier's capability to supply conforming product needs to be demonstrated.
		The requirements specified are aimed primarily at achieving customer satisfaction by preventing nonconformity at all stages from manufacturing through to servicing.
		This standard is applicable in situations when confidence in product conformance can be attained by adequate demonstration of a supplier's capabilities in production, installation, and servicing.
ANSI/ISO/ ASQC Q9003-1994	*Quality Systems—Model for Quality Assurance in Final Inspection and Test*	This standard specifies quality system requirements for use where supplier's capability to perform final product testing needs to be demonstrated.
		It is applicable in situations when the conformance of product to specified requirements can be shown with adequate confidence providing that certain suppliers' capabilities for inspection and tests conducted on finished product can be satisfactorily demonstrated.
ANSI/ISO/ ASQC Q9004-1-1994	*Quality Management and Quality System Elements—Guidelines*	Provides quality management guidelines for use within an organization in the development and implementation of a comprehensive and effective system designed to satisfy customer needs and expectations while protecting the organization's interests.

Standard	Title	Brief description of contents
ANSI/ISO/ ASQC Q9004-2-1991	Quality Management and Quality System Elements—Guidelines for Services	Provides guidelines for the establishment of a quality system for services with the primary objective of preventing unsatisfactory services.
ANSI/ISO/ ASQC Q9004-3-1993	Quality Management and Quality System Elements—Guidelines for Processed Materials	Provides a guide to quality system elements applicable to processed materials, such as bulk products, and discusses means of ensuring effective quality management.
ANSI/ISO/ ASQC Q9004-4-1993	Quality Management and Quality System Elements—Guidelines for Quality Improvement	Provides a set of management guidelines for implementing continuous quality improvement within an organization. Describes tools and techniques for a quality improvement methodology based on data collection and analysis.
ISO/DIS 9004-5	Quality Management and Quality System Elements—Part 5: Guidelines for Quality Plans	Provides guidelines to assist suppliers and customers in the preparation, review, acceptance, and revision of quality plans. Quality plans provide a mechanism to tie specific requirements of the product, project, or contract to existing generic quality system procedures.
ISO 10006	Guidelines for Quality in Project Management	Provides guidance on those quality principles, practices, and quality system elements for which the implementation is important to and has an impact on the practice of project management. Also provides guidance in the application of quality principles and practices to the management of the processes and activities in the project.
ANSI/ISO/ ASQC Q10007-1995	Quality Management— Guidelines for Configuration Management	Provides guidance on the use of configuration management in industry and its interface with other management systems and procedures. This standard is applicable in support of projects from concept through design, development, production, procurement, installation, operation, and maintenance to disposal of products.

Quality Management and Quality Assurance Standards

Standard	Title	Brief description of contents
ANSI/ISO/ASQC Q10011-1-1990	*Guidelines for Auditing Quality Systems—Auditing*	Provides guidelines for establishing, planning, carrying out, and documenting audits of quality systems as well as providing basic audit principles, criteria, and practices. It allows users to adjust the guidelines to suit their own needs.
ANSI/ISO/ASQC Q10011-2-1991	*Guidelines for Auditing Quality Systems—Qualification Criteria for Auditors*	Sets out qualification criteria for the selection of auditors to perform quality systems audits in accordance with ISO 10011-1.
ANSI/ISO/ASQC Q10011-3-1991	*Guidelines for Auditing Quality Systems—Management of Audit Programs*	Provides basic guidelines for managing quality system audit programs. These guidelines can be used to establish and maintain an audit program function when performing quality systems audits in accordance with ISO 10011-1 and ISO 10011-2.
ISO 10012-1-1992	*Quality Assurance Requirements for Measuring Equipment—Part 1: Metrological Confirmation System for Measuring Equipment*	Applicable to measuring equipment. Contains quality assurance requirements for managing, confirmation, and use of measuring equipment used to demonstrate compliance to specific requirements.
ISO/DIS 10012-2	*Quality Assurance Requirements for Measuring Equipment—Part 2: Control of Measurement Process*	Applicable to measurement processes. Contains quality assurance requirements to provide enhanced assurance that measurements are made with the intended accuracy.
ANSI/ISO ASQC Q10013-1995	*Guidelines for Developing Quality Manuals*	This standard provides guidelines for the development, preparation, and control of quality manuals that will reflect documented quality system procedures, as required by the ISO 9000 family of standards, and that can be tailored to suit the specific needs of suppliers of goods and services.

Glossary

Accreditation*: Procedure by which an authoritative body formally recognizes that a body or person is competent to carry out specific tasks.

Assessment*: Another term for quality audit.

Audit*: See *Quality audit.*

Audit program*: The organizational structure, commitment, and documented methods used to plan and perform audits.

Auditee: An organization being audited.

Auditor (Quality)*: A person qualified to perform audits.

CAS number: A number assigned by the Chemical Abstracts Service of the American Chemical Society to identify a chemical.

Certification*: Procedure by which a third party gives written assurance that a product, process, or service conforms to specified requirements.

Compliance*: An affirmative indication or judgment that the supplier of a product or service has met the requirements of the relevant specifications, contract, or regulation; also the state of meeting the requirements.

---

*Reprinted with permission from ISO 9000 Registered Company Directory, published by Irwin Professional Publishing in Fairfax, VA.

Conformance*: An affirmative indication or judgment that a product or service has met the requirements of the relevant specifications, contract, or regulation; also the state of meeting the requirements.

Corrective action: An action taken to eliminate the causes of an existing nonconformity, defect, or other undesirable situation in order to prevent recurrence.

Customer: The recipient of a product provided by the supplier.

Finding*: A conclusion of importance based on observation(s).

Follow-up audit*: An audit whose purpose and scope are limited to verifying that corrective action has been accomplished as scheduled and to determining that the action effectively prevented recurrence.

Inspection: Activity such as measuring, examining, testing, or gauging one or more characteristics of an entity and comparing the results with specified requirements in order to establish whether conformity is achieved for each characteristic. Note: The term *requirements* sometimes is used broadly to include subjective yet required standards of good workmanship.

Lot: A definite quantity of a product or material accumulated under conditions considered uniform for sampling purposes. For a continuous process, a lot is usually defined by a time interval. For a batch process, each batch can be considered a lot. If parts of a lot are later stored and/or shipped under significantly different conditions, it may be necessary to define each part as a separate lot. This definition is based on the broad definition of a process as being any activity that changes the physical or chemical properties used to define the product—blending, mixing, packaging under different conditions, and so on—as well as the usual production processes.

Objective evidence: Information that can be proved true, based on facts obtained through observation, measurement, test, or other means.

---

*Reprinted with permission from ISO 9000 Registered Company Directory, published by Irwin Professional Publishing in Fairfax, VA.

Preventive action: An action taken to eliminate the causes of a potential nonconformity, defect, or other undesirable situation in order to prevent occurrence. A preventive action is taken prior to the actual occurrence of a nonconformance.

Procedure: The specified way to perform an activity.

Process quality audit: An analysis of elements of a process and appraisal of completeness, correctness of conditions, and probable effectiveness.

Product: The result of activities or processes. Product may include service, hardware, processed materials, software, or a combination.

Product quality audit: A quantitative assessment of conformance to required product characteristics.

Purchased product: Material, services, or other types of product purchased from a subcontractor for use in the supplier's process.

Purchaser: Synonym for customer. The 1987 edition of ISO 9001 referred to purchasers while the 1994 revision refers to customers.

Quality assurance: All the planned and systematic activities implemented within the quality system and demonstrated as needed to provide adequate confidence that an entity will fulfill requirements for quality.

Quality audit: A systematic and independent examination to determine whether quality activities and related results comply with planned arrangements and whether these arrangements are implemented effectively and are suitable to achieve objectives.

Quality control: Operational techniques and activities that are used to fulfill requirements for quality.

Quality management: All activities of the overall management function that determine the quality policy, objectives, and responsibilities and implement them by means such as quality planning, quality control, quality assurance, and quality improvement within the quality system.

Quality manual: A document stating the quality policy and describing the quality system of an organization.

Quality plan: A document, specific to each product (or group of similar products), that sets out the quality-related activities for that product. A quality plan should include references to raw material specification and quality control procedures, product formulation, process control, intermediate and finished product specifications and quality control procedures, sampling procedures and packaging specifications, and any other relevant procedures. A quality plan might form part of a detailed operating procedure.

Quality surveillance: The continual monitoring and verification of the status of an entity and the analysis of records to ensure that specified requirements for quality are being fulfilled.

Quality system: The organizational structure, procedures, processes, and resources needed to implement quality management.

Quality system audit*: A documented activity to verify, by examination and evaluation of objective evidence, that applicable elements of the quality system are suitable and have been developed, documented, and effectively implemented in accordance with specified requirements.

Registration*: Procedure by which a body indicates relevant characteristics of a product, process, or service, or particulars of a body or person and then includes or registers the product, process, or service in an appropriate publicly available list.

Root cause*: A fundamental deficiency that results in a nonconformance and must be corrected to prevent recurrence of the same or similar nonconformance.

Service: The result generated by activities at the interface between the supplier and the customer and by supplier internal activities to meet customer needs.

Specification*: The document that prescribes the requirements with which the product or service must conform.

Subcontractor: Any provider of purchased products (for example, raw materials, in-bound goods or services, utilities, or equipment) or

---

*Reprinted with permission from ISO 9000 Registered Company Directory, published by Irwin Professional Publishing in Fairfax, VA.

services that come into the supplier's company (organization, plant, or process). Toll converters, contract warehouses, outside laboratories, packagers, and repackagers are all examples of subcontractors, whether internal or external. Operations internal to a supplier's company may be regarded as subcontractors if they are outside of the quality system defined by the supplier.

Supplier: The organization that provides a product to the customer.

Testing: Determining the capability of an item to meet specified requirements by subjecting the time to a set of physical, chemical, environmental, or operating actions and conditions.

Traceability: The ability to trace the history, application, or location of an entity, by means of recorded identifications.

Validation: Confirmation by examination and provision of objective evidence that the particular requirements for a specific intended use are fulfilled.

> Notes: In design and development, validation concerns the process of examining a product with user needs. Validation is normally performed on the final product under defined operating conditions. It may be necessary in earlier stages. The term *validated* is used to designate the corresponding status. Multiple validations may be carried out if there are different intended uses.

Verification: Confirmation by examination and provision of objective evidence that specified requirements have been fulfilled.

> Notes: In design and development, *verification* concerns the process of examining the result of a given activity to determine conformity with the stated requirements for that activity. The term *verified* is used to designate the corresponding status.

Work instruction: A document that tells how to do something rather than when, where, or with whom; a detailed step-by-step description of a work activity. There are many synonyms in the CPI.

Bibliography

Geoffrion, R. R., R. K. Gill, and G. W. Roberts. *Quality Assurance Guidelines for Research and Development.* Milwaukee, Wis.: ASQC Quality Press, 1994.

Morrow, Mark, ed. *Acronyms and Definitions.* Fairfax, Va.: Irwin Professional Publishing, 1995.

Index

Acceptable subcontractors, 41–43
Accepted order, 18, 19–20
   definition of, xiv, 17
Accreditation, definition of, 135
American National Standards Institute
      (ANSI), vii, 125. *See also*
      ANSI/ISO/ASQC
American Society for Quality Control
      (ASQC), 125. *See also*
      ANSI/ISO/ASQC
   Chemical and Process Industries
      Division, vii, viii
ANSI/ISO/ASQC A8402, xiv, 91–92, 111, 129
ANSI/ISO/ASQC Q9000 series. *See also*
   ISO 9000 series
   cross-reference table, x
   linkages in, ix–x
   revisions in, vii, ix
   usefulness of, xi–xii
ANSI/ISO/ASQC Q9000-1
   description of, 129
   as guidelines, xi
   links within Q9000 series, x
   on organizational roles, viii
ANSI/ISO/ASQC Q9000-2, x, 129
ANSI/ISO/ASQC Q9000-3, 130
ANSI/ISO/ASQC Q9000-4, 130
ANSI/ISO/ASQC Q9001
   comprehensiveness of, xi
   contract review, 17–21
   as a controlled document, 35
   corrective and preventive action, 92–98
   customer-supplied product, 49–50
   definitions in, xiv
   description of, 130
   design control, 24–32
   document and data control, 34–37
   handling, storage, packaging, preservation, delivery, 99–106
   inspection, measuring, test equipment, 72–80
   inspection and testing, 62–69
   inspection and test status, 81–83
   internal quality audits, 112–15
   links within Q9000 series, x
   management responsibility, 1–7
   nonconforming product, 85–89
   process control, 55–60
   product identification and traceability, 51–54
   purchasing, 40–47
   quality records, 107–10
   quality system, 10–16
   servicing, 119–20
   statistical techniques, 121–24
   training, 117–18
ANSI/ISO/ASQC Q9002
   appropriate uses for, xi, 23, 24
   clauses not included in, xi, 23, 24, 32
   as a controlled document, 35
   description of, 131
   links within Q9000 series, x
   revisions in, ix
   servicing, 119

ANSI/ISO/ASQC Q9003
  appropriate use for, xi
  clauses not included in, xi, 24, 32, 47, 54, 60, 120
  as a controlled document, 35
  corrective action, 98
  description of, 131
  inspection and testing, 69
  internal quality audits, 115
  links within Q9000 series, x
  management responsibility, 3
  nonconforming product, 87, 89
  quality records, 110
  revisions in, ix
ANSI/ISO/ASQC Q9004, xii
ANSI/ISO/ASQC Q9004-1, x, xi, 9, 131
ANSI/ISO/ASQC Q9004-2, 132
ANSI/ISO/ASQC Q9004-3, xii, 132
ANSI/ISO/ASQC Q9004-4, 132
ANSI/ISO/ASQC Q10007, 132
ANSI/ISO/ASQC Q10011, 111, 112, 114, 133
ANSI/ISO/ASQC Q10013, 133
Approval
  documents and data, 35–36
  subcontractors, 41–43
Assessment, definition of, 135
Auditee, 113, 114
  definition of, 135
Auditor
  definition of, 135
  training of, 113–14. *See also* ANSI/ISO/ASQC Q10011
Audit program, definition of, 135
Audits. *See also* Internal quality audits
  corrective action, 94
  definitions of, 137, 138
  final inspection, 68
  subcontractors, 42
Authority, personnel. *See* Personnel authority

Backward traceability, 53
Batches, need for definition of, 52
BS (British Standard) 5750, ix
Bulk materials, receiving inspection of, 63, 65
Bulk product, handling of, 100–1

Calibration, equipment, 72–80
Calibration methods, as controlled documents, 35
Capability indices, 19, 43, 122
CAS number, definition of, 135
Cause-and-effect analysis, 52
Certificates analysis, 69, 103

Certification
  auditors, 114
  definition of, 135
  trainers, 118
Changes
  to contracts, 21
  to data, 37
  to designs, 32
  to documents, 24, 37
  ownership title, 67, 100
Chemical and process industries (CPI)
  contract review, 21
  customer-supplied product, 50
  delivery, 99, 105–6
  design control, 23, 27
  handling, 99, 100–1
  in-process inspection, 66
  inspection and test status, 82
  measurement equipment, 71, 77, 78, 80
  nonconforming product, 86, 88
  packaging, 99, 103
  preservation, 99, 104
  process control, 55, 58–59, 60
  product identification and traceability, 52, 54
  purchasing, 40–41, 42, 43–44, 45–47
  Q9004-3 as guideline for, xii
  quality records, 109–10
  regulations, 27
  servicing, 120
  statistical techniques, 122
  storage, 99, 102
  terminology of, xii
  training, 118
Commitment, documentation of, 1
Common carriers, for product delivery, 105
Communication, in design control, 26, 27
Compliance, definition of, 135
Conformance, definition of, 136
Containers, storage, 102, 103
Contamination, product, 100–1, 102, 105
Contract and contract review, 17–21
  between supplier and subcontractors, 17. *See also* Purchasing
  definition of contract, xiv, 17
  design control, 24, 25, 26–27, 32
  final inspection, 68
  process control, 56
  product delivery, 105
  product verification, 47
  records of, 21, 108
  servicing, 119, 120
  statistical tools, 121
Controlled conditions, 23, 57–59
Controlled documents, 34–35

Controls, planning for, 15
Correction, definition of, 92
Corrective action, 91–96
　definitions of, 91–92, 136
Corrective and preventive action, 91–98
　audit results, 114
　management review of, 6
　for measurement equipment, 76
　nonconforming product control, 87
　preventive action, 91–93, 96–98
　in receiving inspection, 64
　records of, 98, 109, 115
　training needs identified by, 118
C_p, 122
CPI. *See* Chemical and process industries
C_{pk}, 19, 43, 122
Critical purchases, 40–41
Custody transfer points, 20
Customer, definitions of, xiii, 136
Customer complaints, 94, 95, 96
　management review of, 7
　servicing for, 120
Customer documents, 34
Customer requirements
　contract review, 18–20
　design input, 27
　statistical techniques, 122
Customer-supplied product, control of, 49–50
　contract review, 20
　inspection and test status, 82
　records of, 108
Customer-supplied test methods, 35
Customer–supplier contract. *See* Contract review
Customer verification, purchased product, 45–47

Data. *See also* Document and data control
　definition of, 34
　purchasing, 43–44
Delivery, 86, 87, 104–6
Design, of packaging, 103
Design control, 23–32
　changes, 32
　design and development planning, 24–25
　input, 26–27
　organizational and technical interfaces, 26
　output, 27–28, 122
　planning for, 16
　records of, 28, 30, 108
　review, 28–29, 108
　statistical techniques for, 122
　validation, 30–31
　verification, 29–30

Design review, 28–29
　definition of, 29
　records of, 108
Development planning, 24–25
Dispatch, 67
Disposition
　nonconforming product, 87–89
　records, 109, 110
Document and data control, 33–37
　approval and issue, 35–36
　changes, 37
　design control, 24
Documentation. *See also* Quality manual; Quality records; Records
　access to, 36
　audit results, 112, 114
　commitment to quality, 1
　contracts, 19
　corrective and preventive action, 93, 94–95
　customer-supplied product, 49, 50
　design control, 24, 27, 28, 29, 30, 32
　handling, 101
　inspection and testing, 68
　internal standards, 75
　nonconforming product, 87, 88
　over-, 56
　packaging, 103
　personnel responsibility and authority, 3
　planning, 15
　process control, 55, 56
　product identification and traceability, 51, 52, 54
　purchasing, 40, 41
　quality system, 10
　servicing, 119, 120
　statistical techniques, 123–24
　storage, 102
　tiered, 11–13
　training, 117–18
Document review, 35, 36, 37
Documents
　compared to records, 33
　controlled, 34–35
　external, 34
　master list of, 35, 36
　obsolete, 35–36
　purchasing, 43–44
　specifications, 44
　uncontrolled, 36

Education. *See* Training
Employees. *See* Personnel
Environment
　design control, 27, 28

Environment—*continued*
  design plans, 25
  measurement systems, 74, 79–80
  process control, 57
  product storage, 102
  during transport, 105
Equipment. *See also* Inspection, measuring, test equipment
  auditing of, 114
  maintenance of, 58, 59
  planning for, 15, 16
  as products, 39
  purchasing of, 40–41
  as a resource, 4
  servicing, 57

Facilities
  auditing of, 114
  as resources, 4
Final inspection, definition of, 67
Final inspection and testing, 66–68
Finding, definition of, 136
Finished products, inspection and test status of, 82
Follow-up activities, 96, 98, 112, 113, 115
Follow-up audit, definition of, 136
Forms, as controlled documents, 35
Formulas, product, 34
Forward traceability, 53

Guidelines
  for internal quality management, xi–xii
  listing of, 129, 130, 131, 132, 133
  for quality planning, 16
  for selection and use of Q9000 series, xi

Handling, 100–1
  measurement equipment, 80
  nonconforming product, 86
Handling, storage, packaging, preservation, delivery, 99–106
  contract review, 20
  delivery, 86, 87, 104–6
  handling, 80, 86, 100–1, 120
  packaging, 103
  preservation, 80, 104
  records, 108, 110
  records of, 101
  storage, 49, 80, 82, 101–2

Identification. *See also* Product identification and traceability
  calibration status, 77–78
  definition of, 52
  need for statistical techniques, 121–23

nonconforming product, 86
test status, 82
In-process inspection and testing, 58, 65–66
In-process materials, 82
Input, to design, 26–27
Inspection, definition of, 136
Inspection, measuring, test equipment, control of, 71–80
  calibration status, 77–78
  contract review, 20
  design control, 28
  environmental conditions, 79–80
  identification of equipment, 74–75
  identification of measurements, 73–74
  planning for, 16
  process control, 58
  process definition, 76–77
  records of, 73, 76, 78–79, 109
  servicing for, 120
Inspection and testing, 61–69
  contract review, 20
  equipment for, 71
  final, 66–68
  in-process, 58, 65–66
  planning for, 15
  process control, 58
  receiving, 45, 58, 62–65
  records of, 68–69, 109
  servicing for, 120
Inspection and test status, 81–83
Instructions, work. *See* Work instructions
Interfaces, for design control, 26
Internal quality audits, 111–15
  corrective action, 96
  management review, 6
  procedures and instructions, 12
  records of, 12, 109
  resources, 4
  training for, 118
  training needs identified by, 118
Internal quality management, guidelines for, xi–xii
International Organization for Standardization (ISO), vii, ix. *See also* ANSI/ISO/ASQC; ISO
Investigation phase, of corrective action, 95
ISO 9000 series, vii, viii. *See also* ANSI/ISO/ASQC Q9000
  history of, ix
  linkages in, ix
ISO 10000 series, xi
ISO 10006, 132
ISO 10012, 75, 80, 133
ISO 10013, 10
ISO/DIS 9004-5, 16, 132

Job descriptions, 3

Labeling
  measurement equipment, 78
  packages, 103
  test status, 82
Laboratory test methods, 34
Lead auditor training, 113–14
Levels, of documentation, 11–13
Life-cycle, product, 9
Lot, definition of, 52, 136

Maintenance, of equipment, 58, 59, 76–77, 79
Management representative, 4–5
Management responsibility, 1–7
  management representative, 4–5
  management review, 5–7
  organization, 2–5
  personnel, authority of, 2–3
  quality policy, 1–2
  records of, 108
  resources, 4
Management review, 5–7
  compared to quality audits, 112
  preventive action, 97, 98
  records of, 12, 108
  statistical techniques for, 124
  training needs identified by, 118
Manufacturing instructions, 12–13. *See also* Work instructions
Master list, of documents, 35, 36
Materials
  planning for, 15
  as products, 39
  purchasing of, 40–41
Measuring equipment, definition of, 72. *See also* Inspection, measuring, test equipment

Nonconforming product, control of, 85–89
  corrective and preventive action for, 91–92, 95
  equipment calibration, 79
  in-process inspection, 66
  prevention from unintended use, 85–87
  receiving inspection, 64
  records of, 69, 88–89, 109
  review and disposition, 87–89
Noncritical purchases, 41
Notification, of nonconforming product, 86

Objective evidence, definition of, 136
Objectives, and management review, 6
Orders. *See* Contract; Contract review

Organization, and management responsibility, 2–5
Organizational chart, 3
Organizational interfaces, 26
Output, from design, 27–28
Overdocumentation, 56
Ownership transfers, 67, 100

Packaged materials, inspection of, 63
Packaging, 103
Performance indices, 122
Performance records, 12
Personnel. *See also* Training
  evaluation of, 118
  interfacing among, 26
  participation in management reviews, 7
  as a resource, 4
Personnel authority, 2–3
  for auditing, 113–14
  for design and development plans, 24, 25
  for design change approval, 32
  for document and data control, 35
  for handling customer complaints, 95
  for inspection, 69
  for process operation, 60
  to release products, 69
  to release purchasing data, 44
  to review nonconforming product, 88
  for training, 118
Pipeline transfers, 105–6
Planned arrangements, definition of, 111
Planning
  design and development, 24–25
  production, 57
  servicing for, 120
Policy, quality. *See* Quality policy
P_p, 122
P_{pk}, 19, 43, 122
Preservation, 80, 104
Preventive action, 91–93, 96–98. *See also* Corrective and preventive action
  definitions of, 92, 137
Priorities, for audit activities, 113
Procedure, definition of, 137
Procedures
  auditing of, 114
  as controlled documents, 34
  documentation of, 10, 11–13, 107–10
Process capability indices, 19, 43, 122
Process control, 55–60
  controlled conditions under, 57–59
  design control, 23, 24
  handling, storage, packaging, preservation, delivery, 99
  receiving inspection, 64

Process control—*continued*
  records of, 60, 109
  for special processes, 59–60
  training for, 118
Process performance indices, 122
Process quality audit, definition of, 137
Product
  custody transfer point of, 20
  customer-supplied. *See* Customer-supplied product
  definitions of, xiv, 137
  nature of, 39
  purchased. *See* Purchasing
Product appearance, 58–59
Product design and development. *See* Design control
Product exchange agreements, 20
Product identification and traceability, 51–54
  customer-supplied product, 49, 50
  in handling, 101
  nonconforming product control, 86–87
  packaging, 103
  purchasing data, 43
  records of, 54, 109
Production schedules, 20, 57
Product life-cycle, 9
Product quality audit, definition of, 137
Product transfers, in-transit, 105
Purchased product, definition of, 137
Purchase orders, 43, 47, 68
Purchaser, definition of, 137. *See also* Customer
Purchasing, 39–47
  inspection and test status, 82
  receiving inspection, 63
  records of, 41, 108
  subcontractor evaluation, 41–43
  verification, 45–47
Purchasing data, 43–44

Q9000 series, vii–xii. *See also* ANSI/ISO/ASQC Q9000
Q10011. *See* ANSI/ISO/ASQC Q10011
Q10013. *See* ANSI/ISO/ASQC Q10013
Quality assurance
  definition of, 137
  standards, listing of, 129–33
Quality audit. *See also* Internal quality audits
  compared to management review, 112
  definition of, 111, 137
Quality control, definition of, 137
Quality management
  definition of, 137
  standards, listing of, 129–33

Quality manual
  ANSI/ISO/ASQC Q10013, 133
  content of, 10, 11–12
  as controlled document, 34
  definition of, 137
  quality policy in, 2, 12
  in tiered documentation, 11–12
Quality plan, definition of, 138
Quality planning, 13–16
  contract review, 19
  design control, 24, 28
  final inspection, 68
  records of, 108
Quality policy, 1–2
  management review of, 6
  in quality manual, 2, 12
Quality records, control of, 12, 107–10. *See also* Documentation; Records
  contract review, 21
  planning, 16
  retention, 109, 110
  in tiered documentation, 11
Quality surveillance, definition of, 138
Quality system, 9–16
  audits of. *See* Internal quality audits
  definitions of, 9, 138
  procedures, 11–13
  quality planning, 13–16
  records of, 108
Quality system audit, definition of, 138
Quarantine. *See* Segregation

Recalls, 65, 66, 109
Receiving inspection and testing, 45, 58, 62–65
Records, 108–9. *See also* Document and data control; Documentation; Quality records
  auditing of, 114
  audit results, 114
  compared to documents, 33
  corrective action, 115
  design control, 28, 30
  handling, 101
  inspection, measuring, test equipment, 73, 76, 78–79
  inspection and testing, 68–69
  nonconforming product, 69, 88, 89
  preventive action, 98
  product traceability, 54
  retention of, 109, 110
  special processes, 60
  statistical control, 76
  subcontractors, 41
  test status, 82

Records—*continued*
    training, 117, 118
    types of, 108–9
Registrar Accreditation Board, 114
Registration, xi, xii
    definition of, 138
Regrading, of nonconforming product, 88
Regulations
    design control, 25, 26–27
    retention times, 109
    traceability, 54
Rejection, of nonconforming product, 89
Release
    before final inspection, 64–65, 68
    by final inspection and testing, 67
    purchase orders, 43
    unintended, of nonconforming product, 85–87
Requirements, definition of, 136
Resources
    management responsibility for, 4
    management review of, 7
    planning for, 15
Responsibility and authority, 2–3
Retention, records, 109, 110
Returns, management review of, 7
Reviews. *See* Contract review; Design review; Document review; Management review; Nonconforming product, review and disposition
Rework, 7, 87–88
Root cause, definition of, 138
Root cause analysis, 92, 93, 95, 96, 114

Safety
    design control, 25, 27, 28
    measurement systems, 74
    placarding requirements for, 103
    process control, 57
    training for, 118
Sampling plans
    as controlled documents, 35
    design control, 28
    elements of, 61–62
    for final inspection, 68
    for measurement equipment control, 77
    planning for, 16
Schedules
    audits, 113
    management reviews, 6
    measurement equipment checks, 75
    production, 20, 57
    record retention, 109, 110
Scope, of quality system, 10

Scrapping, of nonconforming product, 89
Segregation
    for product preservation, 104
    uninspected material, 82
    uninspected product, 86, 101
Service, definition of, 138
Services
    as products, 39
    purchasing of, 40–41
Servicing, 119–20
    equipment, 57
    process, 55, 56
Shelf life, 102, 104
Special processes, 59–60
Specification, definition of, 138
Specifications, 27, 28
    as controlled documents, 34
    documents for, 44
    purchasing, 44
    for servicing, 119–20
Standard operating procedures, 12, 34. *See also* Procedures; Work instructions
Standards
    as controlled documents, 35
    external, 34, 57, 74–75
    internal, 74, 75
    listings of, x, 129–33
    sources for ordering, 125
Statistical control records, 76
Statistical process control, 66, 87
Statistical techniques, 121–24
    capability indices, 19, 43, 122
    contract review, 19
    documentation of, 123–24
    identification of need, 121–23
    in-process inspection, 66
    management review, 7
    for measurement systems, 73
    for preventive action, 97
    process control, 58
    records of, 76
    training in, 118
Statutory requirements, and design control, 26–27
Storage, 101–2
    customer-supplied product, 49
    measurement equipment, 80
    records, 108, 110
    uninspected material, 82
Strategic planning, compared to quality planning, 15
Subcontractor. *See also* Purchasing
    contract with, 17
    definition of, xii–xiii, 138–39
    in design and development plans, 25

Subcontractor—*continued*
   evaluation of, 41–43
   handling, storage, packaging, preservation, delivery, 100
   records on selection of, 41, 108
   selection, 41–43
Subsupplier, xii. *See also* Subcontractor
Supplier
   definition of, xii, 139
   guidelines for, in quality policy, 2
   verification by, of purchased product, 45–47
Supplier–customer contract. *See* Contract review

Tagging, of equipment, 78
Teams
   for auditing, 114
   for corrective action, 95
   for preventive action, 98
Technical interfaces, 26
Technology, as a resource, 4
Tender, 18
   definition of, xiv, 17
Terminology, xii–xiv
   acronyms, 127
   glossary, 135–39
Test equipment. *See* Inspection, measuring, test equipment
Testing, definition of, 139. *See also* Inspection and testing; Inspection and test status
Third-party registration, xi, xii, 138
Tiered documentation, 11–13
Title changes, 67, 100
Tolling, 20, 50
Traceability. *See also* Product identification and traceability
   calibrants, 75
   definitions of, 52, 139
   receiving inspection, 62
   urgent production, 64–65
Tracking. *See* Product identification and traceability
Training, 117–18. *See also* Personnel
   auditors, 113, 114
   planning for, 16
   records of, 109, 117, 118
   as a resource, 4
   servicing for, 120
   in statistical techniques, 123

Transfers, of products in transit, 105
Transporters, for product delivery, 105–6

Uncontrolled documents, 36
Uninspected material storage, 82
Uninspected product storage, 86
Unintended use, of nonconforming product, 85–87
United Kingdom, ix
Urgent production, 64–65

Validated, definition of, 139
Validation
   definition of, 139
   design, 30–31
   measurement processes, 75
   verification, 31
Verbal orders, 18, 19
Verification. *See also* Inspection and testing; Inspection and test status
   compared to receiving inspection, 45
   corrective action, 96
   customer-supplied product, 49, 50
   definition of, 139
   design, 29–30
   effective implementation, 111, 112, 113, 115
   finished product, 67–68
   in-process inspection and testing, 66
   measurement, 79
   planning for, 15
   preventive action, 98
   product release prior to, 64–65
   purchased product, 45–47
   receiving inspection and testing, 62–64
   records, 109–10
   resource adequacy, 4
   special processes, 59–60
   validation, 31
Verified, definition of, 139

Waivers, for nonconforming product, 88
Waste, management review of, 7
Work instruction, definition of, 139
Work instructions
   auditing of, 114
   as controlled documents, 35
   in tiered documentation, 11, 12–13
Workmanship, 58